WHAT OTHERS ARE SA
PERHAPS I'VE SAID TOO MUCH

"I laughed so hard my toolie leaked and I had to change my pants; I now understand I should've been armed with wings. Amazingly funny stories from my favorite man of steel."

-JennieK, Internet Radio Host, TheBrawdcast

"It's a true gift when a writer puts something on paper and makes you laugh out loud. Rodney has that gift and shares it repeatedly in *Perhaps I've Said Too Much*!"

- Gene Lavanchy, FOX Boston

"I laughed so hard I came untucked."

- Bailey Jay, AVN Winner/ Radio Personality

"Rodney Lacroix wins again! His second book, *Perhaps I've Said Too Much*, blows my mind like an exploding Tiffany lamp. It made me excited for my next issue of Chicken Pluckers Monthly."

- Sierra, Co-host of "The Curvacious Bounty of Sin City" radio show

"It's actually possible for someone to make you laugh too hard to the point of pain. That's what Rodney has done again!

- Summer Felix, Author of "Lost & Profound" and "The Right One" series

"There's a lot of boobs in this book. I read it for the pictures. I'm sure it's very good though."

- Neal Mayhem, Broadcaster, Voice Actor, and Writer for Radio and TV

"Hysterical stories that had me crying tears of laughter and pissing my pants."

- Jennifer Garcia, Author of "My Mr. Manny"

"Not quite sure what state program let this lunatic out long enough to write a book, but thank God for government failure. This is brilliant, funny stuff."

- James C. Mulligan, Celebrity Artist and Social Media Whore

Perhaps I've Said Too Much

(A Great Big Book of Messing With People)

Rodney Lacroix

– RCG Publishing –

Published by RCG Publishing because we're good like that – RCGPublishing.com

Physical Book ISBN-10: 0982772041
Physical Book ISBN-13: 978-0-9827720-4-1

Dedication

This book is for all the people who think they can't do something, and probably won't because they never even try.

Hey, you. Yeah, you. Give it a shot.

Do something because you simply feel like it. Get on that stage, sing terrible karaoke, or do the robot dance in the aisle of a grocery store. It's like I tell my kids: "Who cares if you're embarrassed? You may never see any of these people ever again." Whatever it is, just go make a complete ass out of yourself in the name of fun. Be the person talked about when, years from now, someone else looks at their friend and says, "You remember the time we were at that place and saw that guy who did ___? That was awesome."

Be brave. Have no shame.

It works for me.

Thanks

I'd like to thank my loving family, without whom I would probably be sane and wouldn't have been able to come up with nearly half of this crap.

I'd also like to thank cows because steak is my favorite.

Lastly, I'd like to thank all the victims of my shenanigans who may or may not appear on the pages herein. Without you and your gullibility, this book would not have been possible. I guess what I'm saying is that I'm not sorry for any of it because YAY I MADE A BOOK!

From The Editor

When Rodney and I first began discussing ideas for the second book, we had grandiose designs. We pictured threads in each story that tied themselves to the main theme in clever ways. We envisioned bits and pieces of each episode weaving throughout the book in multi-faceted ribbons of life truths that everyone could relate to. We wanted the reader to enjoy the book on another level, above the potty humor on the surface.

But we came up with this instead.

If you've read the first book, **_Things Go Wrong For Me_**, you'll see a lot of similarities. The layout and format are the same, along with the interlude of Draw Somethings. And of course, Rodney still has his same unique style.

Because Rodney's stories are all over the place – along with his mind – it was difficult to combine his previously written stories with new material and still have it match a recurring premise.

We began with "Lying" as the core theme, but expanded it to "Messing With People" because that's what Rodney's style of humor is all about. And since lying is a subset of messing with people (and a prerequisite), the book morphed nicely into what you're about to read.

The first book won several awards, providing much-appreciated vindication for the hard work and long hours I took to put it together. With each award, we screamed, we jumped up and down, we called each other and giggled like little girls.

And it also intimidated the hell out of us. How would we ever top a multiple-award-winning first book? In short, we're not sure we have, but we're sure you'll be entertained.

Because even after the 30th read through, I still giggle at the stories and situations Rod has gotten himself into. And I know you will too.

- Ross Cavins

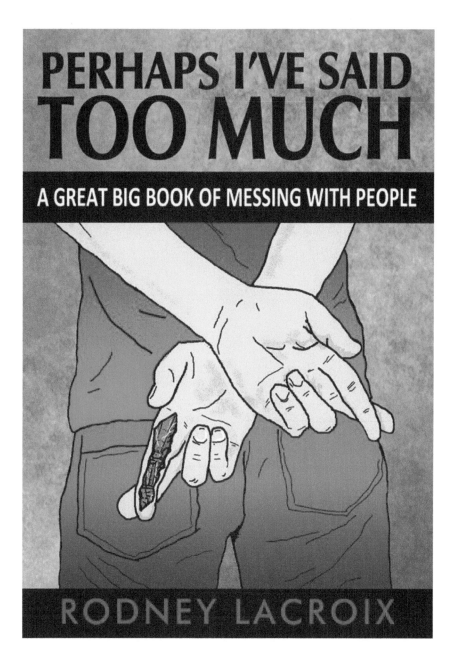

Introduction

I don't know what's wrong with me.

You know? Scratch that.

I actually know of several hundred things that are wrong with me. Most of these things have a clinical name or end with the suffix "ism." In fact, many of them are spelled out in my divorce settlement and labeled as "Exhibits."

Luckily for me, I tend to ignore long clinical names and other things that I can't pronounce. My boss, Mischwa Dashkinamurthy, can attest to this. As such, it's quite possible that the list of things wrong with me numbers well into the thousands. My boss can probably attest to that as well.

As you read this book I'm sure that you'll be adding to this list of mine, so make sure you keep a pen handy. Every time you go, "What the HELL?!" you can just jot that thing down. Truth be told, you will probably get carpal tunnel. I bet somewhere out there is a woman named "Carpal" who is sick of the joke every time a guy sees her vagina. Go ahead. You can start adding to my catalog of issues right now.

Your additions will, in turn, cause the list to grow out of control – much like Doc Ock's self-sustaining fusion ball thingy in Spiderman 2 – and generate a field of gravity so strong that not even light, or you know, a decent book introduction can escape it.

That's actually where the original Introduction went, if you're wondering. It was BRILLIANT. But then the "giant-black-hole-list-of-issues-with-Rodney" happened, so now? Now you get this.

I'm so sorry.

I'm also pretty sure there are plenty of dissatisfied women out there who would be happy to add their own items to this list as well. However, since I'm aiming for a PG-13/light-R rating with this book, we'll leave those items to the historians who will someday write about my legacy. Plus, I think most of the items on the lists from those women will just be synonyms for "sucked" or "too fast" or "liked to have sex while performing interpretive mime dressed as Woody Woodpecker."

You've written down three items already. I can feel it. I can feel it in my BONES.

suggestively rubs hands all up and down body

You see, whenever I do comedy routines or joke around at parties, people inevitably shake their head at me. They're laughing, of course, until they say – and they always say:

"What is wrong with you? Where the hell do you come up with this stuff?"

Then I shrug my shoulders and scream things like "NO WIRE HANGERS!" until everyone gets uncomfortable and leaves. I'm not very good with questions.

Ultimately, I'm left alone with my thoughts. This is where the real magic happens because me, alone with my thoughts, is a very scary concept. It would be way worse if I understood Latin, which is the language most of my thoughts are in. I also float in the air a lot for no reason. In hindsight, I should probably consult a priest about all of this.

As an only child, I had a ton of time to be alone with my thoughts. Not having a sibling to yell at or get into trouble by telling mom and dad that HE was the one who, in fact, painted the dog orange ... actually turns out to be good for one's imagination. Not so much for the dog, though.

Alone time is a great way to build creativity and storytelling, as everything in the world around you is something that you create. Or destroy by fire. Or create and then destroy by fire. In a nutshell, my alone time consisted mainly of making and breaking things, which probably explains my God Complex.

shoots finger lightning and throws 15 Lego mini-figurines across room

Incidentally, this environment is also where most serial killers start their cravings.

I'm just throwing that out there. If you know someone who is an only child, and he's not funny or imaginative, then he's a serial killer, and now you know where the neighborhood cat went.

The more you know.

So shortly after my first book was published, my good friend and publisher, Ross Cavins, came to me about penning a second book.

Ross: "So, what do you want to write the second book about?"

Me: "Uhhhhh ..."

shrugs shoulders

Me: "ARRGH! NO WIRE HANGERS!"

That display was then followed by me doing terribly awkward jazz hands with a forced smile and lots and lots of nervous farting.

Don't worry. He asks me plenty of questions. He's used to it.

What did I want to pen my second book about? Hm. Well, my first book, **Things Go Wrong for Me**, was a compilation of stories about how – as hard as I might try – nothing goes right for me.

I know that's kind of weird because you're saying, "Dude. YOU HAVE A BOOK PUBLISHED," and although it is quite amazing and a crowning achievement for any aspiring writer, I can tell you that this was my first royalty check from my book sales:

CHA-CHING.

"Hey, Hef. I was hoping I could get an invite to the Mansion and nail some Playboy Bunnies because – as I'm sure you're aware – I've published a book that has sold upwards of nine copies. Also, I was hoping you could loan me some gas money."

Hef sheepishly hands me the front door key to the Mansion and a $5 bill

It was right about then that I had an epiphany, which I promptly had removed. This was also around the same time that everyone on Twitter informed me that "epiphany" was not another term for "skin tag."

I then lost several followers because skin tags are gross even if they aren't epiphanies. I'm confusing myself now, so I can only imagine the lack of clarity you're feeling.

Regardless, with the definition of "epiphany" now known, it was about time that I had a proper one. Clearly aware that I may not be able to repeat the same astronomical success as my first book, I began focusing on a new set of life stories that would help people understand just what happens in this brain of mine.

Here's where it gets a little tricky to follow – especially if you're NOT an only child (or don't have anything that can be construed as a non-treatable mental illness).

Because when you're alone 90% of the time, not ONLY do you create an imaginary world, but you also manage to weave that twisted little universe into your everyday conversations with people.

Some people call these "little white lies" or "fibs" or "little white fibs" or "fib lies white little." FYI, if you ever hear someone say the latter phrase, please call 911 because he's probably having a stroke.

Why am I telling you all this?

Because what you are about to read is what happens when one man's solitude is unleashed upon an unwary public. It is, by all accounts, a great big book of messing with people.

When kids or people or people's kids try to engage me in any type of conversation, my response is almost always – invariably – a great big pile of bullshit. Sometimes it even happens without prompting, when my overactive imagination and the voices in my head start taking over, and well, it's all downhill from there folks.

Lies beget lies. What should be simple explanations become epic tales of ridiculous crap. The result? My kids can no longer trust me to answer them truthfully. A simple technical question from a coworker over instant messenger turns into me replying with a bizarre diagram of pyramids. Unattended bananas begin communicating with the corporeal plane. It's confusing now, but you'll see what I mean as you read on and continue jotting things down on your sticky pads.

Trust me when I say that you can take everything coming out of my mouth with a grain of salt ... cross my heart and hope to die, stick some needles in my eye ... I am serious as a heart attack about that.

No wonder it's hard to preach peace in this world. All the metaphors and sayings we have about being honest involve torture and death.

Seriously, if I stuck a needle in my eye every time I didn't tell the truth, I'd look like this:

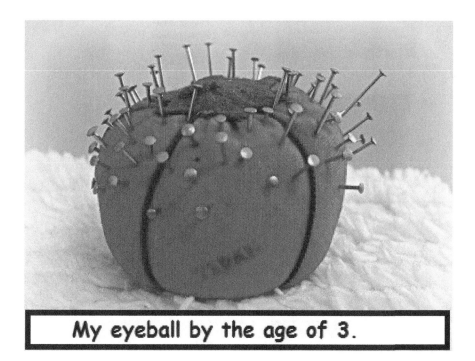

My eyeball by the age of 3.

So I hope you enjoy the tales of how I've gone through life completely driving people insane – either purposely or by way of my challenged subconscious. But don't worry, payback is a bitch, and a lot of times I'm the one saying, "What the hell?" or "Wait. I'm NOT going to jail?!" because it turns out that I'm not the only one who has a penchant for lying and pranking (cheap attempt at foreshadowing).

And as usual, all the stories you are about to read are true. I couldn't make this stuff up.

Or could I?

Perhaps I've said too much.

Liar, Liar, Pants on Fire

I'm a terrible liar.

And I **know** I'm a terrible liar because after I try lying about something the person always says, "You're a terrible liar," and I reply, "AM NOT!" and then I throw a smoke bomb and run away.

I'm not very good with confrontations, either.

Honestly, I'm not quite sure what started my path to liardom ... liarocity ... liaraciousness. FINE, BROKEN SPELL CHECKER HAVE IT YOUR WAY. I'm not sure why I lie. I've always had low self-esteem; maybe it was my way of evening the score by making myself sound better than I actually was.

Looking back, that's silly because I'm kind of awesome. I know that because that's what the Queen of England told me after I saved her dog from the Thames River while traveling Europe with my rich uncle who taught me to fight like Braveheart. He had an eye patch and also showed me how to please all the sexy women using only my pinky and a well-placed belly rub.

As you can see, my lies are like runaway snowballs.

I pretty much lied my way all through childhood, adolescence, and into adulthood (the 'til death do us part' one was the doozy). Even as I was writing this at work, my boss came by and said, "Hey. What are you working on?" and I yelled back, "SPREADSHEETS! I'M BUSY! LAPTOP! TCP/IP!" His eye started twitching and he eventually walked away.

So, yeah. I've told lies. I still tell lies. You'll find plenty of them in the following stories. And I sincerely hope you like them because it's some of the best writing I've ever done.

I know, I know…

I'm still a terrible liar.

THE LIE-ONIC MAN

I was born in 1968 which makes me pretty old, especially if you calculate it in dog years. In dog years, I'm like, 310 which is roughly Mick Jagger's age in regular people years. I'm sorry, I know. You didn't think there'd be math.

As a side note, my first attempt at the opening sentence of this story had a typo in it, so my autocorrect had rewritten it as "ejaculate it in dog years." I don't know how you ejaculate in dog years. I'm guessing it's defined as one orgasm every seven years. This is also known as "marriage."

Continue.

When I was about ten years old in the fifth grade, I was just starting to figure out that people found me funny. I used humor as a defense mechanism against all the kids who made fun of me because I was fat and lazy. Humor was my only defense against bullies because I could barely walk three feet without getting winded and certainly couldn't afford a flame thrower.

Today if you tell your parents about a bully, they call the police. Back in the 70s if we told our parents about a bully, our dads would spend the next two hours teaching us how to surprise-kick someone in the groin while gouging out their eyeballs with a thumb and a dried stick.

Life lessons were different back then. I know several sterile blind men who can attest to that.

Being chunky, I was on the ass end of bullying quite a lot. My response would be to say something funny about them, subsequently humiliating them in front of everyone as they stood there without retort because bullies are stupid. Their eventual response was to look around blankly, furrow their brow, and then beat the piss out of me later during recess while calling me chunky.

Rinse, repeat.

One of my favorite shows as a kid was "The Six Million Dollar Man." I think everyone is familiar with this, but if you're not, it's basically the story of a guy named Steve Austin who gets mangled up in some kind of rocket crash.

And instead of just, you know, pulling the plug, the government decides to invest six million dollars and give him all kinds of bionic parts.

Back then, everyone was all, "OH MY GOD, can you imagine having six million dollars?" but that's pretty much what Bill Gates made in the time it took you to read that last sentence so SCREW YOU, BILL GATES.

I appreciate your purchase.

I hate rich people. Unless this book makes me one of them. Then I like us.

Steve Austin had all these cool powers like bionic eyes that could see really far, bionic legs that made him run fast, and bionic arms that made him super strong. He was like the bastard child of Barry Bonds and Lance Armstrong. We can only guess if they also made his Mr. Wiggly bionic, and if so, there are probably women out there who could really use some "Get Well" cards.

"They found her labia three states away," said the sheriff.

When Steve Austin reaches climax.

Between schoolyard beatings, I honed my comedy skills. They started to take the form of storytelling - a process that took five years to complete since I could only work on it when my bullies got winded and needed snack breaks. The problem with storytelling is that, well, sometimes the story isn't all that interesting and you must embellish a little bit. Just a little. A teeny tiny bit ...

Kind of like this:

I was in fifth grade when, out of the blue one day, a bolt of Steve Austin inspiration struck me, and I began flexing my index finger like it was hurting. For some reason we had indoor recess, but this is New England and snow or rain or sleet or lava rocks falling from the sky are all acceptable weather patterns here on any given day so this was not abnormal.

Since we had indoor recess, the class was milling around and socializing and stuff while our teacher, Mr. Benjamin, sat at his desk.

"Ahhhh," I said, shaking my finger. "Oooh."

My good friend, Tim, came over.

Tim: "What's wrong with your finger?"

I looked around, holding my hand.

Me: "Okay" – *whispering* – "but you can't tell ANYONE."

Tim: "Okay, okay. I won't."

Billy has a secret.

Right here you can see a potential problem, because you cannot tell a child to **NOT** tell someone something.

However, as a child myself, I did not understand this concept.

If you tell a child to keep a secret, there is a 99.99% probability that said secret will be a headline in the NY Times or the top story on TMZ within an hour and a half.

This percentage goes to a full 100% if the secret involves a birthday present for another child in the same household. You might as well give the present to the kid immediately because by the time you're halfway through saying "Don't tell Jimmy what I got him," Jimmy's already cleared a shelf in his room for it.

I motioned Tim closer and he leaned in.

> **Me:** "I got a bionic finger over the weekend."

Tim backed up and leered at me sideways.

> **Tim:** "WHAT?! Shut up."

BRAIN NUGGET

MAKING MY KIDS FILET MIGNON TONIGHT, BECAUSE I HAVEN'T SCREAMED AT THEM FOR PUTTING KETCHUP ON SOMETHING IN A WHILE.

> **Me:** "Seriously. I had an accident on Friday night. They took me to the hospital and sewed a new bionic finger on. It still hurts a little."

> **Tim:** "No they didn't."

> **Me:** "Fine. They didn't."

BAM. There was the classic reverse-psychology technique of taking the ball home with you so others can't play. Want someone to believe something even if it's not true? Pretend you don't care if they believe you or not. I'm pretty sure this is how things like the Loch Ness Monster, Bigfoot, and the Tea Party Movement got footholds.

> **Tim:** "Let me see."

Tim leaned in again, and I closed my fist but held out my index finger to show. As a parent, this is known as the "pull my finger" pose.

Now here's the part where I need you, the reader, to stop what you're doing and turn your palm face up. Now extend your fingers. You see RIGHT where the finger attaches to your palm? It's wrinkly with little pattern that looks like "XXXXXXX." You see that? Well ...

> **Me:** "See? Those are where the stitches were. They attached it RIGHT THERE."

And as I said it, I pointed right to that little XXXXXXX pattern on the base of my finger.

Tim's eyes widened.

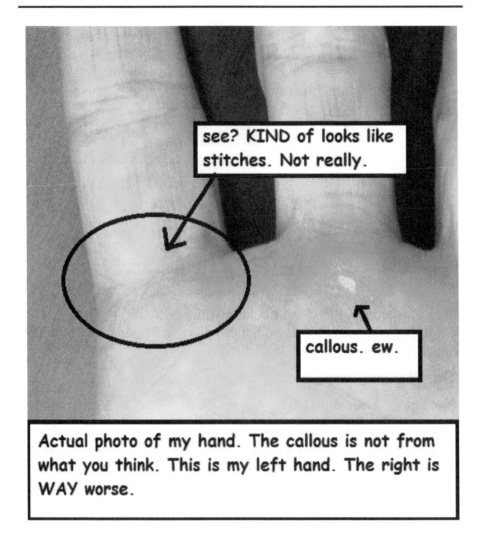

Actual photo of my hand. The callous is not from what you think. This is my left hand. The right is WAY worse.

Tim: "Oh my God. SHUT UP. REALLY?"

Hook and Line ... meet Sinker.

Me: "Yep. And listen ... if you listen really closely, you can hear the gears and levers moving inside when I bend it."

I don't know why I said that. The entire jig could have been up right there, but for some reason the liar in me just had to keep building it and building it, and well, then I was committed to somehow making Tim hear imaginary gear noises inside my fake bionic finger.

The "snowball effect" of my lies, referenced earlier, was in full bloom here, but instead of a snowball, this was pretty much a full-on deadly avalanche.

I held my finger up to Tim's ear and wiggled it a few times.

Tim: "I hear it!"

He ... He heard it?

Um. Ohhhhhhkay. But, hey, cool.

I don't know what the hell Tim DID hear in there, but in hindsight I probably should have had it checked out because – you know – FINGERS AREN'T SUPPOSED TO MAKE CREAKY GEAR NOISES AT AGE TEN.

Me: "Did you? I mean, um ... See? Don't tell anyone."

Then Tim ran off and *swore* he didn't tell the five kids that gathered around my desk minutes later asking to see my bionic finger. Thanks, Tim.

"Make it move."

I made it move.

"Oooh."

"Poke me. I want to see if it feels different."

poke

"OW ARE YOU KIDDING ME?!"

Tip: When asked to poke someone with your "bionic" finger, it is essential to pretty much drive your finger through the person and poke the person standing behind them.

"Pick up this desk using only your finger."

poke

"OW."

The requests got more and more difficult. I wasn't going to be able to pull the ruse off much longer.

Me: "Okay. That's the show for now. Tim, don't tell another person, please."

Tim: "I won't."

30 seconds later

Mr. Benjamin: "Rodney. What is this about a bionic finger?"

Timmy, you sonofabitch.

The whole class turned to me. Well, the whole class minus the five kids prodding me to poke the finger through a half-inch thick textbook. I was on my fourth try, and honestly, my finger was getting pretty sore, so Timmy's betrayal couldn't have come at a better time.

I glanced away from Mr. Benjamin and looked around. The room was a sea of blank faces waiting for an explanation.

As a side note, years later I would encounter this very same classmate reaction after farting in the middle of a deathly quiet Algebra test.

Dammit. I couldn't lie to Mr. Benjamin.

Me: "No. No I don't have a bionic finger. I was just joking."

Mr. Benjamin: "I thought not. Here."

He handed me a slip of paper. It was a note for the nurse.

Me: "What's this for?"

Mr. Benjamin: "You need to have that looked at."

He pointed to my finger ... my previously bionic finger. It was turning purple and swelling ... from the stress fracture I'd just caused while trying to jam it through a damn textbook.

But hey, it was a great five minutes of having a bionic finger.

Imagine what Steve Austin could do to the ladies with that ...

BRAIN NUGGET

FULL BEARDS: BECAUSE IF
NO ONE LOOKS LIKE SHIT,
IT THROWS OFF THE CURVE.

THE NAME OF THE GANG WAS THE "THYROGLOSSALS" AND THEY WERE BAD-ASS

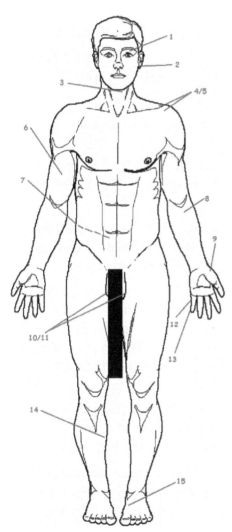

This is obviously not anatomically correct. My arms are WAY bigger.

I have fifteen scars on my body.

Yes.

On my person are fifteen visible signs that I have the physical fortitude, grace, and stamina of a piece of peanut brittle balancing on a marble in a blizzard. Honestly, that may be stretching it a bit.

Some of these scars are from doing things like grabbing pans OUT OF THE OVEN barehanded because vodka makes me stupid. I also have one on my forearm after tearing it open on the breastbone of a turkey at Thanksgiving. That day, I gave thanks for gauze and styptic pencils.

Others are from accidents – like the time I was the cook at a racquetball club and sliced turkey on one of those great big deli slicers. Somehow it didn't occur to me to turn the power switch to the *off* position while reaching across the slicer for the turkey that had just slid off the back.

Please enjoy that visual.

For added effect, while you're picturing it, make a whistling "zzzziinnnnggg" sound. GAH. It was like that scene in "Children of the Corn" where the man's hand goes into the slicer and blood goes everywhere, except there were fewer psychotic children, and more, you know, delicious turkey slices.

I should also take that as a sign I should really avoid turkeys and turkey-related products.

I get scars like social media gets Kardashian updates. In fact, while I was typing that last paragraph I was shot four times by stray arrows.

Nineteen.

Nineteen scars.

The other scars are from surgeries. I have so many that Frankenstein's monster puts on fake scar makeup and goes out as me on Halloween.

Shoulders, bicep, back, hands – I was once in my Orthopedist's office for the third time in six months and asked him if they had a Rewards Card, because for the amount of insurance money they were getting from me, I should at least have been able to cash in for some air miles or a toaster or something.

BRAIN NUGGET

I'M PUTTING DOG SHIT IN THE EASTER EGGS THIS YEAR TO SHOW MY KIDS THE EASTER BUNNY IS NOT AT ALL HAPPY WITH THEIR PROGRESS REPORTS.

Doctor visits in the early 70s.

They didn't, so I remained grounded while holding slices of untoasted bread.

One of my surgeries happened when I was around eight, which probably puts us near 1976. Back then, doctors actually made house calls.

Side Note: Everyone in the 70s wore plaid shirts and green pants, not just doctors.

I have a vague memory of my mother feeling my neck one day and looking concerned. I assume this was probably because she felt a pulse and it was dawning on her that the cyanide she got was counterfeit.

But as she pressed along my neck, she felt around my esophagus and said, "Oh. Oh, I don't like that."

This, of course, is what every boy wants to hear when he's being checked out. Basically, in my eyes, my mother had just told her eight-year-old boy he was about to die a terrible death.

Me: "What?"

Mom: "You have a lump."

Me: "I don't want to die!"

I'm sure my mother did the typical mothering thing, like saying, "it's possible," or "probably," or "hold on while I update your life insurance policy."

In my mind I was already picturing my tiny funeral with all my friends standing around saying, "Who's in there?" because Attention Deficit Disorder was definitely around in the 70s, but we didn't have the benefit of drugs to help us focus. I like trains.

The next thing I remember was being in the doctor's office waiting to have my throat-lump-goiter-death-ball checked out by my physician, Dr. Mansour (pronounced "Man Sore" – and this fact alone should have been a flashing light that no one should ever be seen by a doctor named after syphilis).

I can barely remember Dr. Mansour's face, but I can tell you that he had a pea-green office, because my mind is trained to remember useless facts that have no bearing on the story itself and are only used to pad book pages.

And therein lies my trade secret.

So my mom showed Dr. Mansour this lump that I couldn't see myself because I didn't have throat-eyeballs (which would be so cool). He poked around a minute or two before saying:

Doctor: "It's nothing. It's his Adam's Apple."

Me: PHEW.

Nothing but my Adam's Apple! Also? Yay! I'm a boy!

We left the office and probably got ice cream or something because back then I was a fatty and I ate, like, constantly, and when he said "Adam's Apple" I thought:

Apple = Food, Food = Ice Cream, Apple = Ice Cream.

And that's why to this very day, I think ice cream is a fruit.

Related: I'm terrible at analogies.

My mother, however, was not buying the "Adam's Apple" thing, and off we went for a second opinion. I don't remember that doctor's name OR the color of his office so let's skip directly to the diagnosis:

Doctor: "What we have here is a Thyroglossal Duct Cyst."

Me: "Yay! Ice cream!"

Mom: "What's that?"

Doctor: "It's a cyst growing at the base of his tongue. Right now it's the size of a golf ball. If we don't remove it, it will continue to grow, and he will most likely asphyxiate in his sleep."

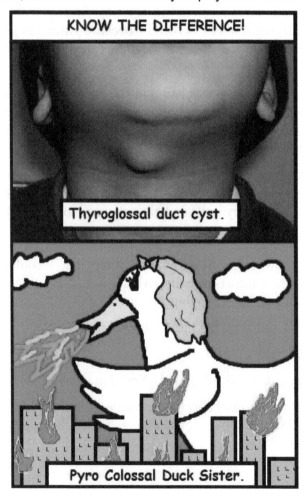

For those doing the math at home:

Adam's Apple = Ice Cream

Thyroglossal Duct Cyst = Death

I like the apple one way better.

Of course, the decision was made to remove the cyst. And so, at the tender age of eight years old, I had my first major surgery requiring anesthetic and stitches. This scenario would play itself out at least five more times over the next 35 years.

Yes, I'm that broken.

What remained after my cyst removal surgery was a scar.

Like, a really big scar that stretched from one side of my throat to the other, just below my third chin but above my clavicle fat.

I had an eight-inch long gash in the *exact area* where people make that "slit throat" gesture. It happened to be just above my ACTUAL ADAM'S APPLE FUCK YOU VERY MUCH, DOCTOR MANSOUR.

The scar was huge. It was ghastly.

It was a great conversation starter.

Kids: "Holy crap. What happened to your throat?"

Being eight years old and finally getting attention for something other than begging for my classmates' Cheetos during lunch period by pretending I was a circus monkey, I came up with the best embellishment I could:

Me: " I was mugged."

I. Was. Mugged.

Yes. That's what I came up with. Scout's honor.

Because nothing says "cool kid" like "mugging victim."

Them: "What?!"

Me: "I was walking down the street and some guy jumped out of the alley. He put a knife to my throat and asked for money. When I told him I didn't have any, he sliced me up."

Then I made that slicing motion with my hand and did that "shquiick" noise to really drive the point home.

It was a sick lie, although, in my defense, the entire mugging charade sounds better than, "Oh. This? A big fleshy growth was here," because there were eight-year-old girls that needed ignoring, and they already thought I was gross enough as it was.

Stupid plaid shirt and green jeans. And ice cream. And hair parted to the side.

God I was gross.

That mugging scar story, though? That made me sound cool. Like I was in an adventure. Kids all over the school asked me about it.

"Really? You got mugged?"

"Were you scared?"

"What kind of knife?"

"Where are you going with my Cheetos, monkey?!"

AH. Attention. The proverbial pot of look-at-me-gold at the end of the rainbow of perpetual lies. Kids were finally finding me interesting, and not just because I could squish my stomach fat together and make my belly button sing "Wheels on the Bus" (a crowd pleaser to this very day).

The story made me legend. I became schoolyard famous. As such, I strung the story out and used it with much success to retain my fame into my middle school years – when we moved to New Hampshire. That's

Actual photo of me, circa 1981. You can see clearly how I would be able to successfully sell a story of being mugged. Also? The girl on the right was hot.

where I made the mistake of further pushing my bad-boy image amongst my new peers by embellishing it EVEN MORE.

It became a gang-related throat slashing.

And no one bought it. Not one single kid.

Instead of being accepted into the ranks of *interesting kids*, I was ostracized as a liar. A bullshit artist. A dipshit.

Kids avoided me. Not even belly button singing would reel them back in.

In retrospect, I probably shouldn't have told my new classmates that I was in a gang while wearing brown corduroys with a Star Wars t-shirt and eating the brown-bagged lunch my mom packed with a little "Wuv U" note inside.

Bad-ass gang members eat steel and spit, not a ham sandwich and an apple.

Apple.

Great.

Now I want some ice cream.

BRAIN NUGGET

DEMAND FOR HOMES IS
CLIMBING SO I DECIDED
TO BE PROACTIVE AND PUT
A 'FOR SALE' SIGN OUTSIDE
MY NEIGHBOR'S HOUSE.

OF PAPER ROUTE MICE AND BOYS

My formative years were spent in an inner-city before it actually became an inner-city. When we walked to school or to the movies or went trick-or-treating with groups of friends, we were always told to be home just before dark. Then the rules got even MORE relaxed once we hit the age of five and our parents could trust us to stay out all night.

The 70s were a much simpler time.

My childhood.

My best friend, Eddie – who was included in my first book as one of my main influences in doing very, very dangerous things that could damn near kill me – had a paper route at age eleven. What this meant was that every afternoon Ed would load up a 40-lb. bag of newspapers across his shoulder, walk around half the city, go right up to people's houses, open their screen doors, and drop them one.

Looking back, this probably explains Ed's chronic back problems. That, plus the fact that he likes to strap cats to his chest on Thursday nights.

TIP: Try to avoid Ed on Thursday nights. You will thank me for this.

Oftentimes, I would go with Ed on his daily paper route. This included most Sunday mornings, when we'd have to walk through the city before the crack of dawn when only other paperboys and cocaine addicts were awake.

It is now painfully obvious to me that not only were the 70s a much simpler time, but it was also probably true that our parents wanted us all dead.

Today, paper routes are mostly done by old men in pickup trucks who may or may not pull over somewhere near the vicinity of your house before throwing your newspaper directly into a gutter or ditch.

So now when I see a strange old man coming around the neighborhood, I assume he's the paperboy. I send my ten-year-old out to greet him and get the paper and maybe ask for candy or offer his daily school schedule and a map of his bus route. (In case I die, I need someone to name as my kids' benefactor. I figure this guy is good as any. Hell, he's got his own van.)

Where he throws my damn paper

FREE CANDY

My paperman.

While Ed and I were roaming the city streets unsupervised, my mom was home cooking and cleaning and slaving over the chores. In retrospect, her tireless work ethic as a stay-at-home mom is probably why I wait to clean my own house or cook anything until she comes over to visit and does it for me while I play Xbox.

Thanks, mom - I love you. Also, my toilets are filthy. See you on Saturday. Bring gloves.

One day, Ed and I were busy – probably blowing something up in the backyard – when we suddenly heard my mother scream. We both looked up, startled, and then, because we were kids, shrugged it off and lit more of my Star Wars and Battlestar Galactica models on fire.

We did this, because no one told me that I would be rich one day if I'd just NOT burned them, and maybe, you know, played with them like a normal kid. Sometimes I look at my $12,000 Visa bill and think of the X-Wing fighters that we doused in lighter fluid and torched and wonder, *"What if ... what if I wasn't such a pyro?"*

That said, we once blew the crap out of a Space Shuttle model using flash powder, smoke bombs, and firecrackers. It was an amazing display of pyrotechnics that would have made Michael Bay gasp. I guess what I'm saying is that sometimes the sacrifice is worth it. Also: Michael Bay, if you're reading this, I'm available for consulting gigs.

We went inside to see what my mom was screaming about and found her standing on one of our kitchen chairs. We had a brown laminate kitchen table and pea-green vinyl chairs so, you know, it's not like she was ruining something from Ethan Allen.

Me: "What?"

Mom: "We have a mouse! A mouse!"

My mother was sobbing. Like, *scared* sobbing. So of course Ed and I laughed because seeing your mother THIS petrified of a mouse is pretty hysterical. We may have even pointed at her. Kids are such assholes.

Mom: "It's NOT FUNNY!"

Me: "Where did it go?"

Mom: "I DON'T KNOW! Rodney go kill it!"

Me: "I don't want to kill a mouse. They're cute."

At this point my mother was scanning the floor like it was covered in scurrying cockroaches with striped shirts on and if she was the first one to spot the "Waldo cockroach" she'd win a million bucks. She was frantic.

Mom: "I will give you $5 if you kill the mouse! FIVE. DOLLARS!"

Cha-ching. Five bucks.

Keep in mind this was the 70s, so having five dollars meant that a kid could buy enough fireworks to blow up toys he hadn't even bought yet. I don't know if we were rich or what, but it was the time of Prohibition and the French Revolution, and because of the Depression, money was scarce.

History was my least favorite subject.

But, hey, five bucks was five bucks, so we had a deal.

Me and Ed: "We'll do it!"

We didn't do it.

Sure, we set up mousetraps and checked them every so often, but nope, no mouse. And every day my mom would ask if we'd caught the mouse, and every day we'd say, *"No,"* because SURE we could lie about it, but then what if she saw the mouse again?

At the very least we'd have to give the $5 back. Or worse, we'd probably be punished and grounded and then we wouldn't be able to blow up more of my toys and OH MY GOD I'D BE SO RICH RIGHT NOW IF I DIDN'T DO THAT.

Seriously. I had all the original Bionic Man and Star Wars figures, and now I'm depressing myself. I'm sorry I've dragged you all into this.

this toy sucked

Imagine all of this on fire and you've nailed it.

About a week or so went by, and Ed and I were wandering through the city streets delivering his papers and deftly avoiding pedophiles as we normally would. One of the houses we went to was a decrepit three-story apartment building. The door was only accessible via a small alley adjoining another shady-looking house, so it was a no-brainer for two young boys to walk right through it.

It's like they say: "With great risk comes great reward." Our great reward was splitting the fifty-cent tip we'd get at the end of the week. We were not very smart children.

It was on our way to the rear of the house through the alley that we saw it.

A mouse.

A dead mouse.

A beautiful, fluffy, dead mouse. Relatively speaking.

We stared at it curled up in all of its rodenty deadness. We glanced at each other, and in our gaze I realized that our pupils had been replaced with the grey-green image of Abe Lincoln himself while little dollar-sign angels floated around our heads.

"chaCHING!" they harmonized. *"chaCHING!"*

These all came up from Googling "money eyes" for a picture to put here. This is why I hate Google.

What we were looking at, people, was not a mouse, NO! It was financial freedom. Really, really gross financial freedom.

Me: "We can't pick that up."

Ed: "No. We'll have to come back with a baggy or something."

Yes, even with greed overtaking us, we were both completely aware of the dangers of Hantavirus. By "Hantavirus" I mean "mouse cooties."

We kicked the mouse over against the wall of the building lest some other person trying to gather evidence of a dead mouse and steal our treasure. Then we covered it with leaves and built a small lean-to over it with sticks. By the time we were done, it looked like the mouse was camping.

The next day, the mouse house was the first one we stopped at. I had found a baggy in the kitchen earlier and put it in my pocket after carefully checking to see that no one was watching. Back then there were no Ziploc bags with seals and all that fancy crap they have today like ergonomic bag grippers, "odorless" plastics, remote controls, and four-wheel capability (I don't shop much).

No, this was a regular, old-school, plastic, stick-your-sandwich-in-and-hope-it-doesn't-fall-out Neanderthal baggy. I still cry sometimes thinking about the "roast beef incident of 1975."

I took the baggy out of my pocket and held it open. Ed grabbed a nearby stick and started flicking the mouse at me because we were boys and boys do really sick shit like this to each other. Eventually he got sick of my

My idea of what the rabies shot looks like.

If this was my nurse, I totally would have picked up the stupid mouse with my teeth.

screaming and started pushing the mouse carcass into the bag. I quickly realized that this was pretty goddamn disgusting and worth way more than $5, since the rabies shots we'd have to get would run us a good $10 or $15, at the very least.

Guiding a dead mouse into a plastic bag with a stick is a lot harder than you'd think. You see, dead mice are pretty stiff (that's what the dead girl mouse said) and don't really move the way you want them to. You push the head into the baggy, and the stiff mouse ass swings away from it. You try to spin the ass part into the baggy, and the mouse head swivels out of it. It's like that saying, "It ain't over till the fat lady sings," if the saying had anything to do with bagging dead mice.

After some struggles we finally managed to get the mouse into the baggy and then dropped it into Ed's sling with all the newspapers, because I sure as hell wasn't carrying it.

As a side note, it occurred to us it would be damn near impossible to trace the black plague affecting the rest of the city to a couple of kids delivering The Eagle Tribune.

BRAIN NUGGET

SPENT FIVE MINUTES ENJOYING THE SMOOTHEST SHAVE OF MY LIFE BEFORE REALIZING I HADN'T TAKEN THE PLASTIC COVER OFF THE RAZOR YET.

We got back to my house, opened the garbage shed, and slid the lid off one of our 55-gallon drums. We found one that was full of trash and gently placed the baggy on top. Angels sang. It was beautiful. It was gross. It was grossly beautiful. But, mostly, it was $5.

Me: "MOM!!"

My mom walked out of the house after a few minutes.

Mom: "What?"

Me: "Come look."

It took some coaxing to get my mom to come down and come look because if there's one thing my mom learned early on, it was "don't trust Rodney." She knew there was only a 50-50 chance I was going to show her something she actually wanted to see vs. her getting locked in the garbage shed while we snuck inside the house to eat cookies.

Mom: "What?"

Me: "We caught the mouse."

Her eyes widened. She peered carefully into the garbage shed, and there, in all its plastic bag rigor mortis goodness was the mouse.

Mom: "OH MY GOD, THANK YOU! Thank you!! How did you catch it?"

Um. How did we ...? Aw, dammit.

We'd been so busy with the planning and execution of this entire charade that we completely forgot to come up with a story on how the hell it got there in the first place. I could feel the look of confusion wash over my face. I looked at Ed. We were telepathically saying, "Oh crap," to each other.

Our pupil Abe Lincolns were rapidly turning back into the black, dead, emotionless eyes of eleven-year-old boys. The five bucks was disappearing from ...

Me: "It was in one of the traps. We took it out of a trap."

Booyah. I totally pulled it out of my ass and saved the day. More importantly, my mom felt relieved. And even more important than that, I was about to get five bucks! Hey-o!!

My mom ran inside and came back out with $5 for each of us.

EACH OF US?! Bonanza!!

**This was pretty much the feeling.
No balloons, though. Or hot chick. :(**

"Thanks mom!" I said as we took the money.

We'd just successfully lied to my mom about a mouse, but it didn't matter. My family was moving to New Hampshire soon and my mom was happy.

Maybe I shouldn't say *happy*. Let's go with *happier*. I mean, I was still her son, after all, and there was only so much joy she was gonna have regardless of how many furry rodents were supposedly out of her life.

But like I said, we were $5

BRAIN NUGGET

SEXY LINGERIE CORSETS:
BECAUSE NOTHING HEIGHTENS
MY DESIRE MORE THAN 15
MINUTES OF UNTYING KNOTS.

richer so that's what mattered to us.

Mom went back into the house to continue cleaning and packing. The days of conspiring with my buddy Ed would soon come to an end.

On the bright side, we WERE moving to New Hampshire, so that meant I'd probably be offered more money from my mom to try to get rid of things like mice, moose, and Bigfoot creatures that were infesting the house.

In the meantime, I'd been asked to help my mom straighten up and get ready for our move. I don't like labor of any sort, but when my dad looped his belt between his hands and did the "snap" thing, I grabbed a toilet brush and started scrubbing.

I'd take rabies shots before getting that damn belt any day.

And then, with just one day to go before the movers came, I was standing over the toilet doing my thing, and I saw the real live mouse for the very first time. It scurried across my feet and ran under the sink, prompting me to scream and jump and piss all over the wall.

Mom: "What's wrong? You okay? OH MY GOD RODNEY DID YOU PEE ON THE WALL!?"

Me: "I'm fine. The wall-pee scared me. You know how seeing pee and poo outside of a toilet horrifies me."

Mom: "I know. I remember the waste-basket poop incident from the pool party. Took you weeks to recover."

Seriously, folks. WEEKS.

Enough chit-chat. That mouse was around here somewhere.

Me: "K. Gotta go."

Then I left the bathroom and bolted from the house as fast as I could. As I ran down the street, I heard the piercing scream of my mother from inside the house, "AAAAHHH! ROOOOOODNEEEYY!!!"

Not turning back, I found Ed and headed to the mall to spend that $5 as quickly as I could. If I turned back, that money was as good as gone – and she couldn't take it away if I didn't have it.

That one time? Spending five bucks to blow up Boba Fett might have actually been worth it.

THE SELF-COMBUSTING LAMP

My mother has always loved to decorate.

This, in and of itself, is not necessarily a bad thing. In fact, if my mother DIDN'T like to decorate, I can tell you that my current house would look like it was inhabited by squatters. Mattress over here, TV balancing on a bar stool with 50-foot long extension cord running through the house over there, three homeless people freebasing cocaine on the floor, no curtains or linens, etc.

So I'm glad my mother likes to decorate.

NOW.

But not so much when I was a pre-pubescent boy who listened to AC/DC and wondered what it was like to kill things.

Growing up, one of my aunts had an antique store. I think my mom felt obligated to buy things from it on the regular to support her sister because I personally can't see anyone making a decent living selling old chairs.

The problem I had was that the things my mother bought were used to decorate my childhood room. Because

The Balls are a nice touch

This lamp comes with 5 extra years of virginity!

what else would be **MORE MANLY** for an eleven-year-old boy than to have a baby-blue, hand-painted Tiffany lamp with pretty white flowers all over it?

"Oh, hello there, testosterone. I know you'd like to come into my room, but there's this dainty lamp in here so you're just going to have to stay outside while – POOF – my penis transforms itself into a vagina."

plays with new vagina for six days straight without taking food breaks

I HATED THAT LAMP.

I hated that Tiffany lamp with every fiber of my tiny little being. I cursed it's feminine curves with every flick of the light switch. But I was only eleven so my curse words were limited to "dammit" and "shit," so most of my cursing sounded like this:

click

Me: "Dammit you shit lamp shitty shit lamp dammit."

My cursing has improved a lot since then.

One day, I was in my room listening to records. For those younger than forty reading this, "records" were big vinyl discs that spun around a turntable while a needle dragged across its surface; the result was music.

I assume this process involved some sort of witchcraft, but then again I'm no expert in the musical occult. Nonetheless, I'm guessing I was probably listening to AC/DC, Accept, The Scorpions, Krokus, Iron Maiden, or Great White (before they got into the business of manslaughter) and **DAMN I MISS THE 80s**.

So there I was, minding my own business, doing what most normal boys did at that age:

Singing in front of my dresser mirror and jumping around on my bed.

Don't act like you've never pretended you were a rock star: invisible microphone, invisible guitar, invisible groupies, invisible crowd cheering you on. While in reality, you were just a completely visible toolbag who appeared to be in the middle of a seizure.

I ran around my room singing like I was on stage in front of 20,000 screaming fans. It was during this musical spasming to blaring rock music that I realized I was missing one critical rock accessory:

Something to swing over my head.

YES. I needed to twirl something over my head in reckless abandon like Roger Daltry. I didn't own a microphone, but if I did, I would have totally **ROCKED. IT. OUT.**

Without an actual microphone to swing around, what was I to use?

My pillow? **NO!** Too fluffy.

My cat? **NO!** Too fluffy. Also? Too loud, and I doubt he'd let me do that to him again without putting up a fight, anyway. SO MANY SCRATCHES.

Then I spotted it.

"Bingo."

There on the floor, in all its shiny goodness, was my belt (of course it was on the floor because I'm a boy and that's where everything belongs).

It was shiny because it had a giant dirt-bike belt buckle because nothing says "sexy" like a boy wearing a belt with a giant brass centerpiece. I began swinging it violently over my head like I was trying to gain altitude with it. At 130 pounds I could be in a belt-induced orbit within minutes.

Hips gyrating. Eyes closed. Mouth screaming. Belt lassoing above my skull like I was a short, singing, mullet-wearing helicopter ...

And that's when it happened.

"HERE I AM ... dun dun dun dun ... ROCK YOU LIKE A HURRIC ..."

Mid-circle, my belt decided to just ...

GO.

Off it went. Out of my hands. I stood – frozen – and watched in slow motion as my belt flew straight toward my homoerotic lamp.

The introduction was made: *"Belt buckle, meet lamp. Lamp, this is belt buckle. Now shake hands as quickly and violently as possible."*

Oh. Oh no.

SMAAAAASH

The Tiffany lamp exploded. It shattered into more pieces than Miley Cyrus' innocence.

Shit dammit shitty shit.

This pretty much sums it up.

The resulting explosion was loud. Really loud.

The lamp's shattered pieces suspended in mid-air like that scene from **The Matrix** ... not wanting to let go of their shiny brass and pewter pinnings ... and then exploded in a violent eruption of epic proportions.

*BOOM *clinkle crash**

I stood there for a moment, stupefied, mouth wide open. My heart thumped. My throat dried up. In the background, the Scorpions blazed.

I resisted the intense urge to break into chorus and instead grabbed the belt – the only evidence – and threw it under my bed. I could hear the "thumpity thump" of footsteps as my mother made a beeline for my room and burst in **without even knocking.**

(She would regret making this same decision years later, FYI.)

Silhouetted by the hall light, she screamed over the music.

Mom: *"WHAT HAPPENED!?"*

I was a boy, so I blurted out the same answer that makes every parent crazy bananas when asked a question that involves "what happened?" or "what are you doing?"

Me: *"I don't know."*

glare

Then ... somehow, my brain managed to form enough thought to speak this gem:

Me: *"It just ... it just **EXPLODED**."*

Sure, mom. My lamp just, you know, exploded.

To further stress this point I made a little *poof* hand gesture.

Good one, Rod. Because lamps tend to explode randomly without warning in the real world.

A short list of things that don't make any sense:

1) Skinny jeans that come in size 18

2) An Eddie Vedder/Bob Dylan duet

3) Spontaneously combusting lamps

4) Brenda from Accounting

In my head, it almost made sense because I knew that if there was something really hot and you poured something cold on it, it would shatter.

I'd learned this from the time we were digging the foundation for the house and ran into a gigantic 25-foot boulder that proved too big to move. My cousin suggested building a bonfire around it, then spraying it with a hose.

After all the adults were finished laughing and calling it the dumbest thing they'd ever heard, asking, "How much have you had to drink?" they ended up burying it, with five feet of the boulder still above ground. My cousin was shamed by the entire family for months and eventually died penniless trying to prove his theory by lighting a mountain on fire in a thunderstorm.

But the science of his claim was there. So why couldn't that happen to a Tiffany lamp sitting on a dresser in the middle of the day? A sudden shift in temperature at the exact spot where my fancy old-lady lamp was sitting would certainly cause it to, you know, BURST INTO PIECES spontaneously.

Right? **RIGHT?!**

Not so much.

> **Mom:** "Um. What?"

> **Me:** "I was just standing here not dancing or singing or doing anything remotely embarrassing and then – BAM – it just went 'pcksshshh'."

> **Mom:** "…"

Sometimes, even when backed by science, terrible-sounding bullshit is still just terrible-sounding bullshit.

> **Mom**: *"That's just great, Rod. I know how you've always hated that lamp."*

> **Me**: *"WHAT!? I love that lamp. LOVE that lamp."*

BRAIN NUGGET

TOLD THE KIDS IT'S TRADITION ON MLK JR DAY EVE TO LEAVE OUT BLACK-AND-WHITE COOKIES FOR HIM WHEN HE COMES DOWN THE CHIMNEY.

In hindsight, that was probably harder for my mother to believe than my theory of the lamp collapsing under its own weight due to unfelt environmental factors and – in essence – trying to become a wormhole.

> **Mom**: *"Mmhhm. Sure you did."*

So it was with relative joy that I witnessed my fancy girlie lamp being scooped up, piece by feminine piece, and thrown in the trash. Forever gone was the stigma of pulling on dainty chains and being greeted with internally illuminated daisies. Every time I had turned that lamp on, I heard a little voice squeak, " ... play with Barbie dolls ... estrogen is your friend ... you will grow to love the taste of penis, just give it time ..."

So lying to my mom about loving that lamp seemed the right thing to do.

Until I came home two days later to find this sitting on my bureau:

You've got to be kidding me.

Mom: *"I know how much you said you loved your other lamp. I tried to find one just like it, but all your aunt had was this."*

Sonofabitch.

And this one wasn't even BLUE.

39

BOUNCE, BOUNCE, BABY

"Hell hath no fury like a woman scorned." – William Congreve

"Revenge is a dish best served cold." – Dorothy Parker

"Beware of a scorned woman carrying gazpacho." – me, just now, having a flash of brilliant inspiration after writing those first two quotes

I love my mom.

My mom has been through a lot of shit. And I'm not even including the time I accidentally thought the box of Ex-Lax in the bathroom was chocolate (the lead story in my first book). If you count that, then she's literally been through a ton of shit (and just about the same amount of laundry detergent).

As you've read, my mother – sadly – has had the dubious distinction of being the target of most of my fabrications and mental torture. How I have lived this long is a testament to her motherly love, my incredibly strong character, and my sincere desire to stay out of prison ... probably.

But, as that first quote goes, hell hath no fury ...

This particular story takes place when I was around sixteen. At the time, I was dating a pretty slutty girl, mainly because she was a pretty slutty girl. Everyone knows that a teenage boy only needs the following things to survive:

BRAIN NUGGET

"DOCTORS SAY LOOKING AT BUSTY WOMEN FOR 10 MINS A DAY IS GOOD FOR YOUR HEALTH." UNLESS THEY'RE YOUR WIFE'S BEST FRIENDS. THEN THE OPPOSITE.

What every teenage boy needs

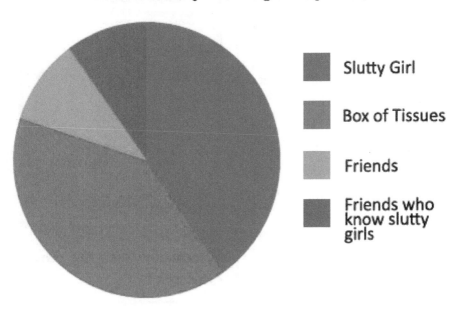

- Slutty Girl
- Box of Tissues
- Friends
- Friends who know slutty girls

FYI: the box of tissues is only for times when the girl isn't around.

This girl in particular wasn't what you'd call a "closet tramp." No. She was one of those flat-out, neon-makeup, leg-warmer-wearing, fifteen-multicolor-bracelet-accessorizing, constant-gum-chewing, mini-skirt-wearing, *"OMG I think your vagina is hanging out"* types of semi-professional penis receptacles.

Have I mentioned she put out?

She was not the kind of girl you brought home to mother.

But because I'm stupid, I did.

The first introduction with her and my mom went something like this *(names have been changed to protect the whorish)*:

Me: "Mom, this is Lucy."

Lucy: "Nice ta meetcha."

My mom looked Lucy up and down.

Bangles. Beads. Big hair.

Ginormous hoop earrings dogs could leap through.

High-heeled ankle-height white boots.

A grimace surfaced on my mother's face. The grimace turned to a look of disgust. My mom glanced over at me, and I could see – very clearly – that she really, really wanted to smack me.

Mom: "Hmph. hello."

It actually went better than I thought it would.

But my mother, being the *mother-of-an-only-child-DON'T-YOU-DARE-TAKE-MY-BABY-AWAY* type of mother that she was, did **not** approve of Lucy.

I actually think she owned this shirt.

I always assumed it was because she felt that "No one was good enough for her only baby boy." But it was probably more that she felt "No one was good enough for her only baby boy, especially a girl who smelled like the entire football team's balls."

Later, my mom told me:

Mom: "I don't like her. I don't want you going out with her."

Me: "Okay."

I said "okay" because I knew it would make my mother happy. I also knew that back then, lying to your mother about getting laid on the regular was pretty normal for teenage boys, so this seemed to be a win-win.

Today, in contrast, kids are open with parents about their personal lives. I'm not sure why this is, exactly, because I think about my kids growing up and doing this stuff, and I want to stick pencils in my ears so deeply I never have to hear about it LALALALALA I CAN'T HEAR YOU STOP MAKING THE HAND SIGNAL FOR INTERCOURSE OHMYGOD OHMYGOD.

sticks pencils in eyes, too

So, of course, Lucy and I kept dating and mashing uglies. And of course, the relationship was unbeknownst to my mother, who remained clueless to the fact that not only was her son getting *sumthin-sumthin*, but that he was getting *sumthin-sumthin* from the same girl that compelled her to disinfect the entire house with bleach after an introductory visit.

Regardless, Lucy and I went out one night to go *"parking,"* which is where you park your car in a secluded area of a street or parking lot – or, in this case, the entrance to the town dump. Now that I think back, that actually seemed appropriate because I really wanted her to touch my junk.

For the younger generation, "parking" refers to making out. This assumes you don't have a Mini Cooper or Smart Car and have room to lean over to the passenger seat without dislocating a shoulder. The result of a successful night of "parking" includes two very tired people, fogged windows, an explanation to a police officer, and a whole lot of car-interior clean-up.

Thank God my car seats were vinyl because I went parking a lot, and it's hard to get stains out of cloth upholstery. I would discover this years later when the dealer docked me $500 on the trade-in value of my Ford Escape because my cloth passenger seat wasn't salvageable and could only be donated to the Human Genome project for help in decoding DNA strands.

Hey. No one said this was an Oprah's Book Club Selection, people.

So, on this night, Lucy and I parked and comingled. Before I knew it, **FIVE hours had passed**, and it was, like, midnight ... and I realized I'd missed my curfew by an hour. Oops.

I still had to drive Lucy home (which was twenty minutes away), meaning I wouldn't make it to my house until almost one in the morning. That was going to be a tough one to explain since I'd told my mom I was going out with friends to a movie that started at eight.

Please keep in mind that this was around 1985 and cell phones were not available for me to perpetuate my lies from a safe distance. I also couldn't text my mom something like: "Lucy DTF. Getting BJ. B home 18r. lol."

Using my infinite teenage wisdom, I decided it would be easier to show up **AT MY HOUSE WITH LUCY IN TOW** and explain to my mother that I did not go to the movies with friends, but that I actually went to the movies with Lucy. *And because I was such a good son*, I had opted to explain the situation to my mom before taking Lucy home, instead of being **extra** late and having my mom worry for no reason.

Because I was a good son.

This thought process should not surprise you people by now.

it worries me how dumb you are.

Had this rabbit been around, this whole thing could have been avoided.

Lucy and I walked into my garage, up the stairs, and into my kitchen. There, in her bathrobe, sat my mother.

A rare moment of clarity presented itself as I realized this was one of the dumbest ideas of my short little life.

I immediately wished for the power of invisibility, or more appropriately, *invincibility* because based on the death stare I was getting from my mom, I was about to be dismembered.

Mom: "WHERE THE HELL HAVE YOU BEEN?!!"

Me: "I ..."

Mom: *"AND What the hell is THAT?"*

The "what the hell is that" question was in reference to Lucy. I could see, based on Lucy's reaction, that she was not used to being referred to as a "that" which is surprising when you consider everything I've already told you about her.

There was an awkward moment of silence as I watched horns, claws, and a set of dragon wings unfurl from my mother's tiny frame.

After a moment, I broke the silence and offered up this gem:

> **Me:** "Well. We went to the movies and we were sitting there and the movie just wouldn't start for like, an HOUR. Then finally when it did we were halfway through it and the **THEATER WAS STRUCK BY LIGHTNING**, so they restarted the movie again, and **THEN** when it was over they gave us passes to go back another time!"

blink

> **Me:** "... and that's why we're so late."

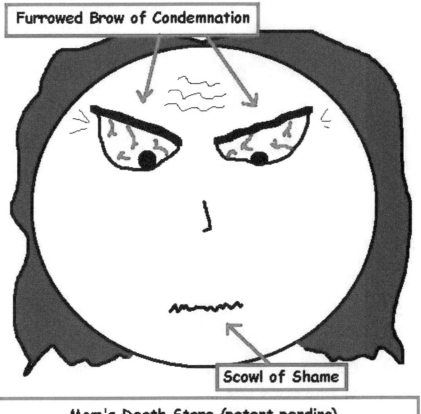

Furrowed Brow of Condemnation

Scowl of Shame

Mom's Death Stare (patent pending)

I looked back at Lucy who was staring at me like *"WHAT THE FUCK WAS THAT?!"*

I couldn't blame her, really. I still don't know where it came from.

I mean, sure, I could have said, "Well, I asked Lucy to go out and time kind of got away from us," but instead, I decided to go with the tried-and-true *movie-theater-struck-by-lightning* approach.

Mom: "OH. Really. Because **I CALLED THE THEATER** and asked them what time the movie got out. Funny, they said nothing about being struck by lightning."

Me: "Oh."

Mom: "You're a LIAR. *I KNOW WHAT YOU WERE DOING*."

I Googled 'busted' for a picture here. This came up. Although not what I was looking for, I'm happy with the results.

Anger and hatred fumed from my mother as she not only realized that her son had been defiled – DEFILED – by a whore, but that he was also lying about it to her face.

If you can imagine, it was very intimidating, and I feared for my physical safety at that point.

I have to tell you, for a teenage boy to feel physically scared by his five-foot tall mother sporting a kinky perm and terrycloth robe pretty much tells you what kind of attitude she was spewing out there.

That's when Lucy made the fateful decision to open her mouth *(not the first time that night, by the way)*.

Lucy: "Well ... we were ..."

At this point it should be noted that Lucy had not quite made it all the way up the stairs from the basement; she was still standing in the doorway at the top step when my mother interrupted her.

Remember that "hell hath no fury" quote at the beginning of this story? Yeah, well, here's where that comes into play ...

My mother cut Lucy short by screaming *"YOU SHUT YOUR MOUTH,"* in Aramaic, then levitated three feet in the air.

Some of this may be embellishment. It was probably more like two, two and a half feet.

True story.

But, yes, my mother screamed at Lucy, and then – with a single hand – *shoved her backwards.*

I watched numbly as my girl/slut went ass-over-teakettle down the stairs, limbs flailing everywhere, bracelets and brightly colored hair scrunchies and condoms and diaphragms and class rings shooting out from all over the place.

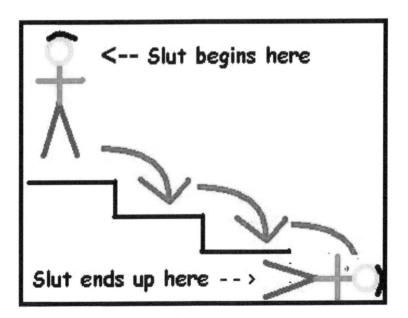

I looked down at Lucy, then back at my mom. I remember not really feeling very dismayed at this girl tumbling down the stairs.

Girls, let this be a lesson to you: If you get yourself into a relationship based only on physical attraction, don't be surprised when the guy has little to no emotion when his mom throws you down a flight of stairs.

I should own a fortune cookie company.

Honestly, what surprised me *most* was my mom's strength. She was a tiny little woman and had just pulled some Lou Ferrigno shit out of nowhere.

Lucy stared up at me from her sprawled position at the bottom of the stairs, a shocked look in her eyes.

Lucy: "Aren't you going to DO something?"

Me: "Um. No. Not really."

Did she not just see my mother levitate, breathe fire, and throw her down the steps using only the Dark Side of the Force?!

This is what my mom did when I only LIED to her. Can you imagine if I got up in her face?! Have you even seen what happens to the victims in "Hellraiser?!"

No thank you, Lucy. No thank you.

I sheepishly looked over at my mother, who was still heaving with disdain and sporting a lovely set of hooves. I made my only smart decision of the whole night: I ran down the stairs, scooped up my vagina in heeled boots, and took her home.

Without saying a word.

Lucy and I never went out again, and when my mother asked about us, I was able to answer with the truth for a change.

In the end, that was probably a good thing because to this very day I remain herpes-free, and Mom hasn't thrown me down a single set of stairs.

Yet.

BRAIN NUGGET

I COULDN'T QUALIFY TO BE A
CONTESTANT ON A GAME SHOW
CALLED, "SO YOU THINK YOU CAN
USE PLASTIC WRAP."

THE BOY WHO CRIED, "I'M INCARCERATED"

When you grow up never being serious, it's pretty hard for those around you to believe anything you say. I'm kind of staring at my son as I'm typing this, because he does this all the time.

Now he's looking back and asking me, "What?" but I'm still typing and staring, and now he's getting really agitated because I'm making my eyes wide like this:

I was not making that face, though. That would take some work.

On an unrelated note, I Googled "eyes wide" for a picture to put here and a ton of naked Nicole Kidman pics came up, so long story short, it's taken me two hours to get this far.

My son takes absolutely nothing seriously, which is a trait genetically handed down from me. I learned this from attending many parent-teacher conferences and when the teacher described my son's behavior, my ex-wife would say, "Gee. Wonder where he got THAT from."

Luckily, my son inherited her calves and her hair so there's hope for him, physically. Notsomuch for my daughter, who got *my* calves and hair. She's beautiful, but she may need to work on her personality to get dates if those traits continue to develop like mine did.

I'm only saying that because I resemble a tiny bald chicken.

As you've gathered already, joking around has been my modus operandi throughout my entire life. Joke at funerals? CHECK. Joke at weddings? CHECK. Joke at job interviews? CHECK. Joke on dates? OF COURSE.

The reason you joke on dates is because being funny is the number one thing women look for in a man.

Luckily they are able to look past the fact I'm unemployed and banned from funerals and weddings within a hundred miles.

BRAIN NUGGET

I HAVE MANY REGRETS, BUT NONE BIGGER THAN WHAT I DID FOR THAT KLONDIKE BAR.

The number two and three things women look for are great calves and a full, luscious head of hair, and I'm going to stop right there because I'm bumming myself out.

Now to the actual story (ADD is my copilot) ... Once when I was seventeen, I took my mom's Mercury Cougar out on a date with my girlfriend.

I don't remember why exactly I took my mom's car on this date, but I assume it was because my kick-ass 1970 Oldsmobile had its engine out or needed a new carburetor or just had a new coat of vinyl protectant put on the front seat and that stuff has a tendency to stain a set of corduroys.

Whatever the reason, the girlfriend and I headed out in style, and boy were my friends gonna be jealous!!

After the date – complete with awkward heavy petting and a severe case of blue balls – I dropped her off and headed home.

I had to drive about a half mile on a two-lane road with a 40-mph speed limit, and then turn through a bunch of back roads to get to my house. I live in New Hampshire so "bunch of back roads" here is unnecessary since the state first allowed paved roads circa 1985. Even then I think the person who suggested it was stoned to death.

BRAIN NUGGET

THE PEOPLE UP THE STREET ONCE YELLED AT ME TO MAKE SURE I PICKED UP MY DOG'S POOP, SO TO PROVE IT I'VE BEEN PILING IT ON THEIR STEPS.

In fact, I can remember the uproar when someone wanted to open a McDonald's in my town. They said it would "ruin the landscape," and God forbid we move that rock and cut down a couple of trees so I can enjoy a tasty Big Mac. Town planners are assholes.

My route home looked like this picture below:

There I was, tooling down the main road just after leaving my girlfriend's house when a cop passed me going the opposite way.

Did I forget to mention that the town's Police Station was on this main road? Don't answer that. I just scrolled back and looked. I didn't. Unless you count the last paragraph. Then I've totally mentioned the Police Station that this cop was probably heading to ...

Until I blew by him going about 60.

On went his flashers.

He started making a U-turn.

In telling you what comes next, I must first remind you that I was seventeen with two big blue balls of backed-up testosterone. As such, my brain was already non-functioning from lack of blood flow, so my pubescent instincts and adrenaline kicked in ... AND I FLOORED IT.

Thinking quickly – and I use that term loosely – I shut the lights off and pressed the pedal harder.

"YES! I WILL GO DARK AND THEY WILL NEVER SEE ME HAHAHAHAHA!"

The speedometer zoomed:

61 ... 61-½ ... 62 ... 62 ... 62-½ ... OH COME ON!

Mercury: *Fine purveyor of the world's slowest luxury cars costing under $8000 that you probably shouldn't try to outrun the police in.*

The police car was taking longer to make the U-turn than I expected, but I'd missed my first turn towards home because I was busy keeping an eye on him.

All I had to do was make an extremely sharp hairpin U-turn way up ahead without dying, then it was smooth sailing back to my house where I'd be safe.

Yes, safe. I thought – like I think most people on "Cops" do – that once you get to your house they can't touch you. Like you have diplomatic immunity on your own soil because you pay Bank of America $2000 a month to stay there.

You can pull into your driveway, stand there, moon them, and stick your tongue out at them, and they can't do a thing because, you know, police have no jurisdiction whatsoever past your mailbox.

Cop: "Dammit, Jim. He made it to his driveway. Let's go grab some coffee and a box of krullers."

So with thoughts of a clean getaway and safe haven, I turned the corner while shaded in darkness and peeked behind me.

Oh. Look. HE'S RIGHT BEHIND ME THIS IS AMAZING. AMAZINGLY BAD. SO BAD SO BAD SO BAD.

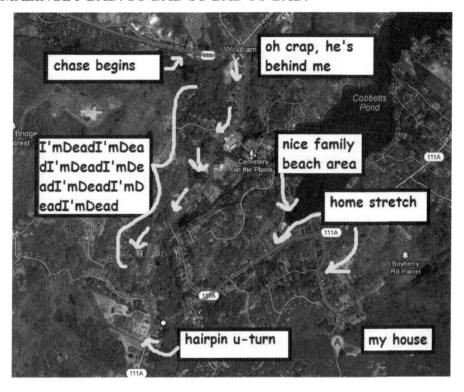

At this point I have no idea how fast I'm going, but I've turned the lights back on because, well, my mom's car is white, so that was a pretty stupid idea to begin with. Also, the car was making those same lines behind it that the Enterprise does when it goes into warp speed, so I wasn't fooling anyone.

I passed cars on a double-yellow two-lane road, flying as I approached that hairpin turn I mentioned earlier, but I was so close to freedom that I could taste it. It tasted like cherry. My girlfriend used way too much lip gloss.

I cranked the wheel to the left, made the hairpin turn, and looked out my driver's side window, realizing there was now a WHOLE BUNCH of police cars chasing me. The reality was setting in:

1) I was totally going to get caught.

2) I was going to jail.

3) Guys in jail like men with small calves and very fine hair.

4) I should have taken the Oldsmobile.

The epiphany suddenly hit me that I had to stop, so I slammed on the brakes, going from 60 to 0 in roughly two feet. Say anything you want about Mercury automobiles, but their brakes are top-notch. I highly recommend using whatever brake pads and rotors they use if you ever plan on being in your very own car chase. The preceding was not a paid advertisement.

I sat on the side of the road, suspended in the seatbelt with my eyes googily stretched out like Slinkies from my sudden stop. I looked up to see a State Police car fly over the hill in the opposite direction. Aw, cute! The local police had invited some friends over to the WORST. PLAYDATE. EVER.

The police car chasing me that started the whole thing slammed on his brakes and went skidding into the woods on the opposite side of the road. Apparently, my town's police did NOT use Mercury brake pads.

I jumped out of the car and put my hands on my head probably yelling "I SURRENDER" or "DON'T SHOOT" or "PORK IS THE OTHER WHITE MEAT!" (so true).

The next thing I remember was being cuffed, dragged into the cruiser, and put into the back seat. They did that nice *please watch your head* thing because even though I broke at least fourteen laws and could have killed ten people during the chase, they wanted to make sure I didn't get a bump because little head bumps are nasty things.

Cop: "Rodney, really?"

I looked up and realized **I knew the arresting officer personally**.

Also? He had a passenger. **She was a friend of my girlfriend's older sister.**

See this? This is why small towns suck. I couldn't even come up with a lie about a shoot-out or anything because almost everyone I knew was involved in the car chase. I would'nt have been surprised if several of my neighbors, teachers, the local pharmacist, and that weird kid named Wayne with the terrible stutter and Marty Feldman eyes from elementary school emerged from the other cars.

Poor Wayne. Stutter + Marty Feldman eyes = hookers for life.

Mind racing, I began working on how to get out of my jam. I was hoping to play on the fact that I knew the officer who'd just been chasing me for the last three miles.

Make up something good, Rod. Make it believable. Make it ...

Me: "Kim. Kim broke up with me."

Ah, I went for the "girl dumped me" excuse. I was focusing on the sensibilities of the officer. Maybe he could relate to another man who has had his heart crushed in such a way that his only recourse would be to commit a crime involving high speeds and several dozen policemen.

With his heartstrings sufficiently pulled, the officer would then immediately let me go on my own recognizance. We would high-five and regroup at the next meeting of the He-Man Woman Hater's club, beers in hand.

SPOILER ALERT: He did not let me go. Maybe he was gay.

By the time we reached the police station, it was close to one in the morning. I had no idea what they did with my mom's car, but they took my belt so I wouldn't hang myself.

I was sad about the loss of my belt, mainly because the same belt buckle that had heroically survived the Tiffany lamp tragedy of years earlier was still attached to it. We'd been through a lot together, me and my dirt bike belt buckle. Someday, belt buckle and I would look back on this and laugh like old friends in therapy together.

Officer: "Make your phone call."

In a room with three cops watching, I reluctantly called my house. I knew my parents would be asleep. They would also be sharpening knives after the call so they could skin me alive once they got hold of me.

Ring ... Ring ... Ring ...

Phone picks up ... fumbling ...

Dad: "mmhpphh ... hello."

The next thing that came out of my mouth actually sounded like I'd won $100 on a scratch ticket. I'm not sure why my tone was like this other than the fact that it's how I roll, even in terrible situations such as this.

Me: "Hi dad!"

Dad: "mmph ... what, Rodney. What?"

Me: "Guess where I am?"

Yes. For some reason I found it to be a great idea to make my father – who would want to kill me in roughly thirty seconds – GUESS WHERE I WAS in the middle of the night ... and the right answer be "jail."

Dad: "Rod," *–he was slowly waking up–*"Cut the shit. I don't know where you are. Where are you?"

Me: "Where would you never ever never ever want me to be ever. Especially at one in the morning."

Dad: "I don't know."

Me: "I'm in jail."

Now here? Here is the part I was talking about. This is where EVERYTHING from fooling around at funerals and weddings and joking on dates and never ever taking anything even remotely seriously catches right up to you:

Dad: "Very funny. Come home. It's late."

click

My father. Hung up. On me. For my one phone call from jail. He hung up on me. I looked at the cops and held the phone out to them in my handcuffed hands.

Me: "He hung up."

They LAUGHED.

Cop: "Try again."

Ring ... Ring ....

Dad: "What?"

Me: "Dad. I'm in jail. You need to come get me."

BRAIN NUGGET

> TEXT FROM DAUGHTER:
> "I AM IN LUNCH DETENTION."
> ME: "FOR WHAT?!?"
> DAUGHTER: "TEXTING."
> ME: *FACEPALM.

Dad: "OH MY GOD will you just come home."

click

ARE YOU KIDDING ME, DAD?!

Me: "Um. He hung up on me again."

It was quickly becoming clear that, (a) I should probably take things a bit more seriously in the future, and (b) I should tell the truth a smidge more often, and (c) I was going to die in jail, probably from complications of anal fissures.

One of the officers grabbed the phone and dialed. He did not give me the phone this time.

Cop: "Hello. Mr. Lacroix? This is Sergeant Willis. Your son is at the police station. He's been arrested. You need to come make arrangements for his release. Yes. Okay. Thank you."

Then he hung up and told me my dad was on his way. He led me to a cell where I had to sit and wait for my father to come and murder me. The cell was cold and red, probably so the blood stains wouldn't ruin the ambience. It also had a stainless steel toilet in the corner that looked like your ass would freeze to it the moment you plopped onto it.

Now I'm picturing putting my tongue on a frozen pole. Now I'm picturing it's not a frozen pole but a frozen stainless steel toilet. Now I'm grossed out.

Still chuckling, the officer looked at me and gave my belt back. Sure it probably broke protocol, but he figured I had bigger issues than trying to figure out how to hang myself. On the bright side, I'd have a great story at school and could embellish some of it because the only people who actually SAW me do all this was the officer and his passenger.

Sure. I could add in some details.

> " ... and then I heard the whirring blades of a police chop ... I mean, Blackhawk helicopter overhead."

> " ... and so now the hood has holes in it from where they shot at me with a 50-caliber machine gun."

> " ... I counted at LEAST two grenade blasts."

And that's when, shortly after the cell door clanked shut, a voice called out from the cell across the hall:

"R-R-Rodney Lac-c-croix? Is th-th-that y-y-you?"

I glanced over to see a man with Marty Feldman eyes smiling back at me. It was Elementary-school Wayne; he'd just been booked for soliciting prostitution.

I hate small towns.

MAHAL-UH-OH

It's the middle of winter in New England, and I'm sitting in my living room watching MMA fighting on TV as I write this story. As a side note, I think I would make an excellent MMA fighter if I was younger and tougher and didn't get winded easily and actually wanted to fight. Or knew how to. I forget where I was going with this because I get distracted easily.

* leaves for 2 hours to go make a snowman *

MMA actually has some bearing on this story, which took place circa 1988. I was in my second year of college, living at school, and making terrible life choices as most college kids do.

Luckily, most of these choices are a blur as they were the direct result of funneling six-packs of beer.

Another side note: I'd like to think that it's divine intervention we black out when we get too drunk. All I know is that after some hard college partying involving multiple episodes of passing out, I simply stopped making noise when I farted. Nothing. Like a man blowing smoke rings. I have my suspicions as to why, but am happy remaining blissfully unaware of the facts. I'm pretty sure God looked down at the verge of something terrible happening to my drunk ass

My MMA fighting strategy.

and thought, "You know, it's probably best he doesn't remember what's gonna happen next."

Psst...munkey...I haz 'roofied u and now give u bumsex

..if my dog attended my college parties.

The worst of these bad choices involved the crystal clear waters and the black sand beaches of Hawaii. It was for those beaches and that water that my parents decided to abandon their only child and take a two-week vacation.

Yes. They left me behind.

They left a college student of legal drinking age to fend for himself ALONE in a house with a full liquor cabinet while they went to Hawaii for two weeks.

As you can probably see from this foreshadowing, my parents were also guilty of making terrible life choices. But theirs were not nearly as bad as mine because I know for a fact that my father made lots of noise when he farted. True story.

With the prospect of my parents gone for two weeks, I started floating around the idea of having a party for my small group of college buddies and friends. We got the word out around campus while focusing on recruiting as many of the girls from school as possible. My school provided degrees in nursing and dental programs so it seemed like a no-brainer to have as much vagina as possible at the party that also knew how to check your prostate, fill your cavities, or – in the best case scenario – do both at once.

I Googled "bad idea" for a picture to put here and this came up.
I fucking love Google.

We had a lot of *maybes*, because the party was being held during Spring Break when most of the kids with money went to places that didn't have two feet of snow on the ground. Like what my parents were doing.

OHMYGOD they were such jerks. I'm still bitter.

The prospect of having none of these "maybes" show up initiated the following brainstorm (and by *brainstorm* I mean *terrible idea*):

Me: "Let's put up flyers."

And so we did. We put party flyers up all over the school. We stapled them to bulletin boards in every dorm. I even handed flyers to friends in my hometown to pass around. About the only people who didn't know about the party were my parents, who left a few days before the planned event.

Dad: "Be good. Be careful. AND NO PARTIES."

Me: "I will. I will. No, no parties. Promise."

Party Day

My friends from college began arriving in the early afternoon and the house prep began. We had absolutely no idea how many people were going to be showing up, so the first order of business was that I needed to make sure the house was clear of valuables, breakables, and – most of all – stocked full of booze.

I also made sure my waterbed was full, because there just might be some sexy time going on later that night, and waterbeds with low volume make balance and thrusting and jumping and chicken dancing very tough to do.

Related: Sex with me is terrifying.

The main thing I needed to do was move things. We decided that my parents' bedroom was the place where all the breakable stuff was going to live, and then I'd just mark the room as **OFF LIMITS**. Easy peasy.

My parents fine china and crystal? *Moved.*

The glass curio cabinets housing my mom's Hummel collection? *Moved.*

This terribly blurry photo was taken in my living room where you can clearly see the orange decorations and that Marc was the only guy who knew how to dress for success.

The bright orange furniture that looked like it came from the Brady Bunch house?

Nah. Fuck it. It's bright and orange. That stuff should have been burned YEARS ago.

The statue?

Ah. The statue.

In my living room was a small statue of a little cherub holding a stupid cornucopia because nothing says "classy" like a statue of something in your house holding a horn.

The top of the statue sat on a round base, which was also part of the statue, and had tiny little cherubs holding grapes all around it. When I took the top of the statue off, I looked at the base and thought:

Me: "Ah. Well, someone can use the base as a seat."

So we kept the base of the statue to be used as a seat if someone needed somewhere else to plop their inebriated ass, other than our bright orange Brady Bunch furniture. We also decided to leave the two corduroy recliners out in the family room because they also screamed "classy."

drunk person's bum goes here

See? BRILLIANT IDEA.

The recliners were sitting on either side of an antique pewter lamp with round decorative white glass globes that came from my aunt's antique store. At this point you can probably gather that no one in my family knows anything about interior decorating, or really, how anything should look in general.

With the house prepped, my five college buddies and I sat around and waited for people to come.

And waited.

And waited.

By about six p.m. I was starting to get worried no one was coming to the party, so as the host and person directly responsible for the safety of others and sanctity of the dwelling I was entrusted with by my parents, I got utterly shitfaced.

I was blotto. Like, Lindsay-Lohan-at-an-open-bar kind of drunk.

Back then I weighed about 130 pounds so getting me to that level of hammered basically took half a beer. I was so drunk that I don't remember when the first wave of people started showing up.

I do remember, though, that I didn't recognize any of them.

And before I knew it, my house was wall-to-wall people. I honestly wish this was an exaggeration, but from one wall to the other to the other to the other was a sea of humanity. Terrible, underage, drunken humanity. Of the estimated 120-150 people milling around my house, I maybe knew twenty of them. The rest were kids from – apparently – the rest of

this seems accurate.

the country, and even then I think some of them flew in from other continents because I distinctly remember someone speaking Latvian.

OMG. Those. Stupid. Fucking. Flyers.

My kitchen.

I will now present to you snippets I remember from the party because to this day that's all that remains in my mind:

- One of my friends, Mike Hunt, passed out in a chair. Mike had taken the night off from listening to his name repeatedly called out over airport loudspeakers, and was instead slumped in a chair, head back, and arms folded. This, in and of itself is not exciting, except that he passed out while tipping back on the rear legs of said chair. Thus, he was performing an amazing balancing act while unconscious. Making this even more exciting was that directly behind him was a sliding glass door. And making this even MORE EXCITING was that just outside the glass door was a ten-foot drop to my backyard.
- Everyone was taking bets on whether or not Mike was going to fall backwards and crash through the door. I placed my own bet because, aside from the music, there wasn't much entertainment.
- I interrupted an orgy in my bedroom. I got yelled at when I flicked the light on and three heads popped up from the floor on the far side of my

bed. No one was actually on my bed, and strangely, no one was doing a chicken dance.

- I made out with some chick and asked her to stay. I didn't know her, nor had I ever seen her before. She said she would stay. This is how Ebola starts, people.

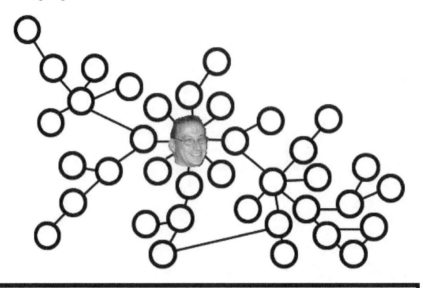

Typical chart on the wall of the CDC

- My friend Rich – who provided the entertainment for the evening – found me and said his CDs were stolen. Keep in mind this was back in the late 80s when CDs were just coming out, and no one could figure out how to play them on record players or how to fit them into tape decks. But Rich had a CD player and brought it with him and became the first recorded case of felonious compact-disc theft in the continental United States.
- I made that charge up.
- And most of all, I remember the fight.

The Fight

The climax of the night began when my friend Kevin barged into my room while I was mid-chicken dance and said, *"DUDE. Some guy just punched me in the face!"*

I don't know who punched Kevin.

What I DO know is that Kevin turned around, went back out into my family room, and punched the guy back, right in the side of the head. This, in turn, started a fight that is typically only seen in the stands of European soccer matches. FYI, if you watch European soccer matches then we will probably never be friends.

"*FIGHT!*" somebody yelled.

I ran out of my bedroom just in time to see fifteen people crash over my dad's recliner. They smashed the antique lamp just as another group of kids crashed over the second recliner.

Fists flying, the fight spilled out into our breezeway which was a small room with a storm door and about six windows. Well, *five* windows after my friend John was PICKED UP and thrown through one. The mass of pugilists then smashed into the metal storm door, buckling it and pushing it open where everyone then continued the fight out in my snow-covered walkway.

"EVERYONE OUT! EVERYONE OUT!" I screamed.

And that's when I called the police.

Yes. I called the police on my own party.

By the time the cops got there, my house was empty except for my college buddies. Tire tracks were six inches deep in the snow on the front lawn. The house was in tatters. Luckily, all of us who remained were legal, so the cops didn't press charges or do anything. Probably because they knew that when I woke up in the morning ...

HOLY CRAP SHIT POOP FACE LOOK AT MY HOUSE!

You know the footage of the nuclear tests they used to do in Nevada? When the house gets blown back from the shock wave and then is completely leveled when it's sucked back in? I would have gladly taken one of those houses in trade.

The two recliners looked like chaise lounges that'd had a piano dropped on them. The round glass globes on the antique lamp were shattered to pieces. The storm door looked like a bull had run into it. The window in the breezeway was gone. GONE.

And then there was the statue.

You remember that great idea I had of using the base of the statue as a seat?

Well, yeah.

SOMEONE USED THE BASE OF THE STATUE AS A SEAT.

As such, the base completely sheared apart at midpoint. One of the little cherubs had broken off, and hundreds of tiny plaster shards were EVERYWHERE. I don't know where the cherub actually went; I think he grabbed his beer and fled with everyone else.

And he never came back after sobering up so I was left with a giant, broken, cherub-free base. You know the song, "Two Out of Three Ain't Bad?" Well I'm here to tell you it IS bad when the two out of three things Meatloaf is singing about are my mom's statue cherubs.

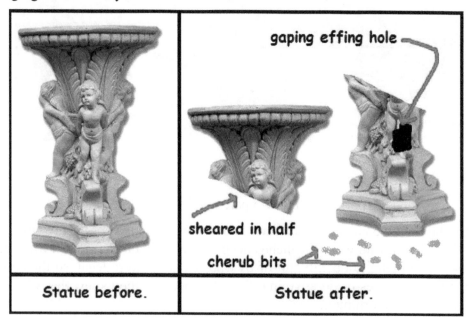

gaping effing hole

sheared in half

cherub bits

| Statue before. | Statue after. |

My parents were due home in five days.

The cleanup began immediately. My friend Stal went to work on the recliners, but the metal bars inside were bent and couldn't be straightened. The furniture was moved back, the rugs were cleaned, trash was thrown out.

I spent the next few days buying windows and replacement screens for the breezeway. If you know me, I'm not handy. I am less than handy. If a cartoon was made of my life, it would be named, "Rodney the Useless Explorer," and when I called for Map and Backpack, we'd all stand around while contractors did the actual work because that's way easier.

The best I could do for the round globes on the antique lamp was to replace them with octagonal ones because my aunt only had that type in stock. I know what you're saying, "What kind of cut-rate antique store only has octagonal pewter lamp globes?" Preaching to the choir, my friend. Preaching to the choir.

The day before my parents came home, the snow melted. And that's when I saw the glass. And the blood. Yes, the blood.

My walkway looked like Hansel and Gretel had both turned emo and decided to leave a trail of their own plasma. I'd forgotten that my buddy had been thrown out the window and my front yard turned into the battle scene from "Braveheart" minus the accents and kilts and guy with leprosy.

So with 24 hours until the folks came home, I bleached blood splatters off of my front walkway in ball-freezing temperatures while looking for tiny bits of glass.

See? This is why I couldn't be a serial killer. Don't get me wrong, I could probably kill someone. It's just that the whole "getting rid of evidence" thing is exhausting. Plus, harsh cleaners dry my wonderfully supple hands.

BRAIN NUGGET

WITH ALL THAT SHIT IN HER BACKPACK, IT MUST TAKE DORA FOREVER TO GET THROUGH AIRPORT SECURITY.

Oh ... the statue?

Well, when I placed the sheared halves of the base together, IT STAYED IN PLACE. The problem was the missing cherub. Where the cherub used to be was just a great big hole that turned the base into a really cool-looking piggy bank.

So with the base being held together by friction and some other fancy scientific principle, I decided it was best to turn it around. I shifted the base so the cherub hole faced the other side and then pushed it up against the wall.

There. Fixed. Cherub hole out of sight, cherub hole out of mind.

CLIP-N-SAVE:
How to repair a statue pedestal!

1. Gently place broken top on broken bottom

2. Don't sneeze

3. Face gaping cherub hole to wall

4. Pray.

Mom would NEVER see it.

Also? I said "cherub hole." I know you caught it, too. So dirty.

And then – shortly after the house was adjusted - my parents came home.

"Hey! We missed you!"

"I missed you, too!" I replied. But I didn't. I wanted them to stay away longer because I was sure I'd forgotten something. Then they showered me with t-shirts and things carved from coconuts. Because nothing says "Sorry for abandoning you, son" like "here's a coconut monkey head."

After a few minutes, with my super stylish "Hang Loose" t-shirt and hand-crafted coconut primate skull in hand, I said, "I'm going to my room to watch TV" and left.

Not five minutes later ...

Knock Knock

Mom opened the door.

> **Mom:** "Rod? Did you ... um ... did you change the globes on the lamp?"

You've gotta be kidding me.

FIVE MINUTES. THEY'D BEEN HOME FOR FIVE MINUTES AND MOM HAD ALREADY FOUND SOMETHING?!?!? Who remembers what kind of globes are on a stupid lamp?!?

You know, besides my mom.

I had not expected to start spinning lies that soon, but she was forcing my hand. Frantically, my mind raced for some type of plausible explanation.

> **Me:** "Um. Yeah. I knocked it over when I was vacuuming and one of them broke."

> **Mom:** "Oh. Okay."

BAM. Crisis averted. Add extra points for mentioning house chore.

jazz hands

The next morning, my dad's yelling woke me up. This was not unusual because my dad liked to yell and – in his defense – I was his son, so he really had no choice. But this time was different.

> **Dad:** "WHAT THE GODDAMN HELL HAPPENED TO THE DOOR?!"

He was talking about the screen door. The mangled screen door. I was able to replace the broken screen, but the metal on the lower part looked like Thor used it for battering practice. If you picture a person's face as his hammer then this analogy is pretty accurate.

> **Me:** "Oh. Yeah. I was shoveling the steps and tripped into it. I'm sorry."

> **Dad:** "Jesus. Be more careful next time."

jazz hands

Then my dad looked up and ...

Dad (gawking at the front yard): "OH MY GOD WHO DROVE ON THE LAWN?!"

puts jazz hands away and runs like hell

Later that night we were getting ready to watch TV when my dad tried to use his recliner. The image of this still makes me laugh until this very day because whenever he'd try to push the top of the recliner back, the bottom would start to come out. But the metal was bent so the bottom would come out skewed and crooked and tilted like it'd just had a stroke.

Then the whole chair would get stuck until he pulled in the arm a little bit, and the end result looked like he was sitting in a chair designed by Picasso on a bender; his legs were flailed to the left, and his upper body was turned to the right, and that probably explains all his back problems.

Every time my dad pushed that chair back, it came out tilted and angled. He got frustrated and said under his breath, "This goddammed chair."

Eventually, the post-party discoveries began to slow down.

A month passed and I began to relax. That was the last of it.

The last of it, that is, until the day I came home from school and was greeted by the statue base sitting in the doorway, the giant cherub hole staring at me.

BRAIN NUGGET

My mom had turned it around and discovered its gaping, cherubless void.

WHEN IT COMES TO RELATIONSHIPS, THE MAIN THING I WANT IN A WOMAN IS MY PENIS.

I didn't see that one coming. It never occurred to my teenage mind that my mom would actually MOVE things when cleaning. I guess I'd hoped that the missing cherub would one day become statue-sick and return to the home from whence he came. I still wonder where he is. Is he lost out in the cold? Hungry and alone?

Maybe I should put up some flyers.

PITCHING A TENT IN MY FRONT SEAT

knock knock knock

My eyes still closed, I heard the faint noise of someone knocking on ... something ... in the distance.

But, man, was **I TIRED**, so whatever. I drifted back to sleep.

knock knock knock

The knocking seemed louder. I squinted my eyes open a tiny bit and tried to prop myself up.

rustle rustle

Um.

Rustle, rustle?

I opened my eyes and glanced around me, my head still in a fog.

"What the hell?"

Let's back this story up a bit.

I went to college.

throws ice water on your unconscious body

Not only did I go to college, but I graduated with a degree in Architectural Engineering. Yes, there was math involved. Yes, I had to study physics. Yes, it all really, really sucked. But would I do it all over again? Absolutely not.

The fact that I have a degree in Architecture comes as a surprise to anyone who has ever seen me try to hang a picture or bang nails into something. Most times, the nails end up bending immediately and it looks like I just made a diorama of tiny confused spikes. I am also pretty sucky at taking measurements. I assume other people can't measure either, which is why I give my penis length in millimeters. Then it sounds like it's enormous, especially if you whisper the 'milli' part.

If you think I'm exaggerating about this lack of skill, please note that we had a blizzard in New England as I was writing this. I took a tape measure into my yard and stuck it in the snow, then posted the pic of the measurement to Facebook. Here's what I got for responses:

Like · Comment · Unfollow Post · Share · Edit

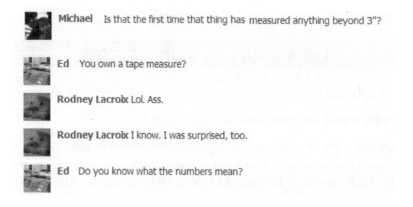

Michael   Is that the first time that thing has measured anything beyond 3"?

Ed   You own a tape measure?

Rodney Lacroix Lol. Ass.

Rodney Lacroix I know. I was surprised, too.

Ed   Do you know what the numbers mean?

Please note that these are really good friends of mine.

Well, WERE.

My ineptitude of doing anything even remotely *constructiony* aside, I managed to get through college in one sexy piece, free of any International incidents.

Please note that "International incidents" does not include the time my friends and I headed to Montreal for Spring Break and took photos with strippers in the middle of the street at three a.m. and pretty much covered the city in our vomit and urine. Everyone around us was speaking French and none of us could understand it, so we walked down the streets in a drunken stupor just saying "schnitzel" over and over.

Me: "Dah. Ungh schnitzel schnitzel?"

Stal: "Oooh, ya. Schnitzel schnitzel schnitzel!"

That went on for three days.

So college came and went without a hitch. Then, right around the corner from my 21st birthday, one of my college buddies decided to have a graduation party. I was invited because I'd been told that I put the "part" in "party." The actual part I put in is a trade secret, but suffice it to say it's why I'm no longer allowed at the local Chuck E. Cheese.

There was a live band and booze, and all my other friends were coming: Spike and Dano and Stal and Pepe (nicknamed "Pepe" not because he was Mexican, but because he had droopy man-boobs like someone's grandpa). We were pretty psyched because you know ... LIVE BAND AND BOOZE.

I conveniently lived in the next town, so I drove to the party in my 1970 Oldsmobile Cutlass. That car was super badass: black, two-door, red racing stripe down the hood, big fat tires, dual exhaust, and – to top it all off – a license plate that read "Rowdy."

This is "Rowdy."
Guys, if you show your woman this picture, please allow her a few minutes to compose herself.

It was fast. It was loud. It was a total chick magnet. When you're 5'3" with a mullet and no real future to speak of, you need all the help you can get.

So I washed and waxed that baby and did what I could to make it louder and faster. I did this because, as far as compensating for a small penis goes, Corvettes were way out of my price range.

Today, I drive a Honda Civic that has an iPod port and gets good gas mileage.

Life is cruel.

Instead of bucket seats, the Cutlass had a big bench seat in the front. For those automobile purists who say, "Aw. Buckets would have been sweet in that car," they are missing the entire paragraph before about the car being a chick magnet, and the fact that *climbing into the back seat* just to get blue balls sounds exhausting when we could totally dry hump in our Jordache Jeans RIGHT HERE.

My car interior always smelled like smoldering denim and melted rivets.

So I got to the party and parked my car on the side of the road at the edge of the woods.

That's me. Oh, laaaaadiiiieees!!

I feel 'edge of the woods' is redundant here seeing as I said the party was in New Hampshire. Some of us commute to work on goats that we just had sex with. It's pretty rural.

About an hour into the party I was completely and utterly hammered. I remember seeing a band and talking with my friend Chris who was trying to bang this chick I had tried to bang months earlier. However, I had limited success with her because, as a general rule, girls don't like me once I start talking to them.

Plus, Chris was better looking than I was. In retrospect, I'm not sure why I hung out with him because he was obviously cockblocking me the entire time.

"Sex hindsight is the worst hindsight of all" – Confucius, probably.

And that's about the time the blackout happened.

Back to the beginning ...

knock knock knock

I heard the faint noise of someone knocking on ... something ... in the distance. My eyes were closed and I was lying on my side, but I managed to lift my head almost an inch.

But, man, **I WAS TIRED**, so I drifted back to sleep.

knock knock knock

The knocking seemed to get louder. I squinted my eyes open a tiny bit and pushed to prop myself up.

rustle rustle

Um.

Rustle, rustle?

KNOCK KNOCK KNOCK

I pushed myself up and slowly turned my head to the left. A bright light shone in my face, damn near blinding me. I shielded my eyes with my hand, and that's when I realized I was sprawled across the bench seat in the front of my car. As I sat up, I felt ... things ... falling around me.

Leaves.

Under me. Around me. On me.

Leaves everywhere.

And branches. Leaves and branches. I was COVERED IN LEAVES AND BRANCHES INSIDE MY CAR.

"What the frigging hell?" I said, spitting out leaves and twigs like someone had stuffed my mouth with Grape Nuts without the milk.

They were everywhere.

"Open the door," a voice boomed from outside the car.

It was a cop.

"Ah, crap."

I sat up completely behind my steering wheel. A branch poked out from under my shirt sleeve. Dried leaves cascaded from my hair. Various sticks and debris protruded from the collar of my shirt.

Dramatization of how I awoke in my front seat.

I opened the door.

> **Cop:** "Why don't you come with us."

> **Me:** "Okay, am I under arrest?"

> **Cop:** "No. We're just taking you into protective custody so you don't drive."

> **Me:** "Okay."

> **Cop:** "Um." – *squinting* – "Why are you covered in leaves?"

> **Me:** "Uhhh. No idea."

I really didn't. I had not one goddamn clue.

I was still super drunk, so I barely remember going to the Police Station and having to call my mother and father to come get me. I rode home with my mom while my dad drove my car in front of us. It was terrifying watching him drive it because (1) it was my car, and (2) it was MY car, and (3) have you seen how awesome my car was and MY DAD WAS DRIVING IT?!

> **Mom:** "I'm disappointed in you. I really am. And why are you covered in leaves?"

> **Me:** "I DON'T KNOW!"

We got home, I passed out, and the next day I called my buddy, Spike – also an architectural engineering major.

Spike: "What happened to you? Where did you go?"

Me: "Ugh. I must have passed out in my car because I woke to the cops knocking on the door. They put me into protective custody."

Spike: "OH YEAH. You passed out alright. Then we covered you in leaves."

Sonofabitch.

Me: "You covered me in leaves? Who does that? I was BURIED in them."

And then came this explanation from Spike. Which I guess was as good as any I could have heard:

Spike: "When you woke up, we wanted you to think you were in the woods."

blink

They wanted me to think I was in the woods.

Lying on the vinyl front seat of a car. Surrounded by my steering wheel, radio, instrument panel, and seat belts.

"Let's add leaves," thought all my architect peers, "he'll think he's in the woods."

Me: "That makes sense."

And that, people? That is why you leave the practical jokes to folks who might know how to pull them off. Also, you should prank people with things that might actually work and not confuse the absolute crap out of the person and/or police officers taking said person into custody.

As an added recommendation, you should probably not try to come up with a prank while completely out of your mind drunk because – in that state – anything sounds good.

This also outlines a great example of why you should get a second opinion on the building plans for your new house, because people with architectural degrees aren't the swiftest bunch in the world.

And now that I think of it, maybe get some schnitzel while you're at it.

I'm a Workaholic ...
if 'workaholic' is short for
'working on becoming an
alcoholic'

"I love my job."

- nothing I've ever said, ever.

You know that feeling you get from a job well done? The pride and sense of accomplishment you feel from focusing all of your efforts into your job?

Yeah. Me neither.

I'm not a fan of working.

This is probably evident in the fact that I'm writing this at two in the afternoon while "working from home." If my boss is reading this, then please know I'm totally joking, and I'm working really, really hard[1] on my current job tasks[2] to make the company[3] money and be successful.

Long story short, I've held a ton of jobs over the years. I've been a dishwasher, chef, line cook, ski salesman, land surveyor, septic system designer (no shit), architectural draftsman, internet security specialist and – lastly – a software quality engineer.

Alas, the title of "porn star" still eludes me, but I'm hoping one of my books hits and a scandal ensues and L.A. comes calling. I actually think I'd be good at it as long as people didn't watch and I was in the film by myself in pitch blackness. Also, the films should only be limited to 30-second clips, because stamina is not my strong suit.

---

[1] Not hard at all
[2] At creating the introduction for Chapter 2
[3] me

porn producer slowly replaces phone on hook

No matter what job I've held, though, I've at least tried to make it entertaining for those around me, which I do by entertaining myself first.

Whether it's messing around with coworkers for my own enjoyment or acting like an asylum patient via instant message, I try to take advantage as much as I can.

People say you should have a job you love. Well, I love making myself laugh. Unfortunately, this usually involves making others miserable or confused, but – hey – you can't argue with people who make up sayings.

So I do what I can to make things unorthodox in the workplace. Take, for example, the fact that my latest job adopted Google Mail, which allows you to put up a picture alongside your email profile.

These profile photos, in turn, are sent along with all our company email correspondence. As such, you'll find that most people attach professional looking pics, or – in extreme cases – the really ugly people do Glamour Shots to make themselves look better (Tip: We are not fooled, Mrs. Sasquatch).

Instead, I do things like this:

Rodney Lacroix

Software Engineer

Rodney Lacroix

Software Engineer

Rodney Lacroix

Software Engineer

Rodney Lacroix

Software Engineer

Rodney Lacroix

Software Engineer

Ugh. Joanie. Seriously, Chachi. What were you thinking?!

Rodney Lacroix

Software Engineer

I change this up once a week or so. I really thought I'd catch hell for the Ron Jeremy one, but then realized that if I did get in trouble it meant that Human Resources would have to admit they knew the guy was a porn star, and well, ***catch-22***. Or *catch-69* if we're discussing in adult film terms.

See? It all comes back to me working in porn.

Then?

Then I'd probably love my job.

...

WARNING: The stories you're about to read are true. The jokes? True. The actors portraying the people making the true jokes in the true stories? Not actors, but also true.

That doesn't make sense. I mean they're real people. My own confusion? Palpable. My correct usage of the word "palpable?" False.

Screw it. What I meant to say was, "Try this shit at your own risk." Where the risk I'm talking about is your unemployment, inability to get a job anywhere else in the civilized world, and possibly jail time.

I've always liked pulling pranks on people, but frankly, I'm not that good at getting away with it. The intent is there, but more often than not I pull a gag off on someone, and then get bagged by them later on.

Then I swear off ever doing it again. Until the next day.

So sometimes I decide to not pull a gag off, and instead, leave it on. It's sexier that way. Plus I like those latex suits where just the boobs stick out. What? Nothing.

The worst thing is when my victim retaliates with something involving spiders. I can't stand spiders even a little OHMYGOD WHAT'S ON MY SHOULDER?!?!?

Okay. I'm back. False alarm. It was my shirt.

BRAIN NUGGET

People know spiders are my kryptonite, so they often get even with some sort of "spider joke'" (no such thing). Then I kill them.

> IN NEW HAMPSHIRE,
> 'BLACK HISTORY MONTH'
> IS A PRETTY BIG DEAL
> FOR THAT GUY.

So feel free to use these pranks yourselves. But if your victim enacts revenge by killing you, it's your responsibility to bail them out of jail. Not mine.

On a related note, I don't understand how life works.

THE MAIL FRAUD STORY OF 1988

I have to preface this story by saying that before I did anything noteworthy (still waiting), I worked in a civil engineering firm. I wasn't civil OR an engineer OR even firm so the irony itself is spectacular here.

I'll give you a moment to breathe it all in.

This civil engineering firm was run by two brothers. They were modern-day giants. I wish I was joking, but the shorter of the two, George, was 6'5", and the taller one, Paul, was 6'8".

With me at 5'3" on my tiptoes, you can best imagine a day at that office by recalling the scene in "Fellowship of the Ring" when Gandalf first shows up at the Shire. I'm playing the role of Frodo, the firm is my house, and both owners are Gandalf.

Or how about the scene in Part Two with Treebeard when the hobbits are sitting on his shoulder as he's walking through the forest? Although in my defense, stuff like that usually only happened at the Christmas party.

I miss that place.

One of my best friends and coworkers at the firm was Jim. We passed the time by messing around and playing jokes on each other instead of, you know, contributing anything of real value to the company.

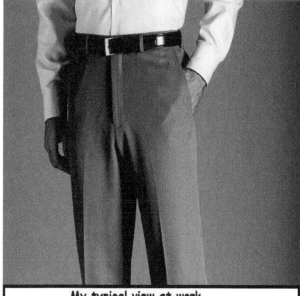

My typical view at work.
Although this probably explains all the raises.

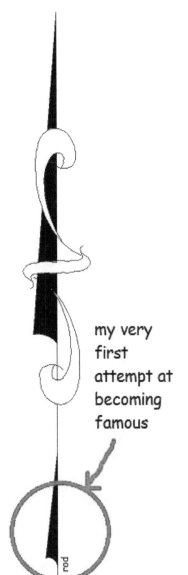

my very first attempt at becoming famous

For instance, there was the time we wrestled in the common area of the office and I threw Jim *through* a wall. My bosses insisted I spend my Saturday patching it.

The joke was on them, though, because my home improvement skills are so bad that the final product made the wall look like it had contracted leprosy.

Then there was the time when Jim was in a bathroom stall taking a dump, and I stood at the sink, lobbing soaked paper towel ball after soaked paper towel ball over the wall at him. It was all fun and games until I heard him say, "Hey ... now THAT'S a funny color," and looked down to see Jim's hand protruding from beneath the stall door, holding a piece of toilet paper with a schmear of his brightly colored green poop on it. And that, people, is how to stop a bathroom stall wet-paper-towel-attack dead in its tracks.

Jim and I shared an office in the basement. So glamorous. The room was "L" shaped, and I sat with my back to Jim as we did our daily work drawing septic systems on computers.

SIDE NOTE: We were once commissioned to do the official town map and – since I was drawing most of it – I put a tiny little "rod" at the tail end of the North Arrow. It was displayed in pizza places, the library, town hall. You name it.

And every single time I saw it I would point out the tiny little "rod" on the arrow. Right now, the pre-pubescent boy in me is dying to not point out "'tiny little rod," but I guess I just did it anyway. Have I mentioned I'm drinking?

Oh. I'm drinking.

Our building also shared space with a guy named Chuck. Chuck designed chicken processing facilities. Contrary to what I first thought chicken processing facilities were, they are NOT a place where chicken police fill out the paperwork after arresting a chicken criminal. I don't want you to be lost in all of this.

Chicken Processing Facility design is an actual thing. Like, if you were Colonel Sanders or Jim Purdue or Popeye, you would need a place to kill the chickens. And Chuck? Chuck designed those places.

I have no idea what those designs entailed. I imagine that, in a parallel universe, chickens go to the movies and watch "Chicken Saw" where two roosters wake up, shackled in a basement. A loudspeaker crackles and a voice commands one rooster to escape, while the other is told to simply kill the first rooster or his hen and chicks will die. The camera pans out to the man speaking into the microphone. It is Chuck, the mastermind of the entire thing.

This is what I pictured chicken processing facilities to be like. This is also why I avoided Chuck like the plague. Sick bastard.

On another side note, I will send his name and address to PETA right now for a million dollars. How about it, PETA? Think about the chickens.

end PSA

This guy received all kinds of weird mail. But what struck my eye one day was a small package of index cards he'd thrown out. They were perched on top of the trash, still wrapped in clear cellophane.

Dozens of magazine subscription cards.

I took the pack out of his trash, and opened the cellophane.

My eyes lit up.

Chicken World

Chicken Processing Weekly

Chicken Industry Magazine

Beheaders Monthly

It was a treasure trove of WHAT THE HELL I CAN'T BELIEVE THEY MAKE MAGAZINES LIKE THIS. I was amazed. There had to be at least forty different cards of weird chicken processing fetish periodicals.

Holy. Crapola.

So I went to my office, grabbed a pen, and signed my coworker Jim up for every. Single. One of them.

Every one.

Address? *Check*. Jim's phone number and extension? *Check*.

Oh.

"Bill me later?"

CHECK.

Then I mailed them.

On a related note: I am the biggest asshole friend ever. Actually, it might be more accurate to put "friend" in quotes right there. I just did.

Then the waiting game happened. One week. Two weeks. Maybe even three, when one day, the receptionist – Julie – came down with our mail. As usual, I had nothing because I was maybe twenty years old and had no interest in anything other than porn.

Not much has changed.

Julie dropped off the mail and a few seconds later:

Jim: "What the fuck?"

I turned.

Jim held up a magazine, his face a muddled mess of confusion. He frowned.

Poultry World.

I burst out laughing. I couldn't help it.

BRAIN NUGGET

COLD-CALL FROM A RECRUITER: "WONDERING IF YOU WERE OPEN TO NEW OPPORTUNITIES."
ME: "AM I HAVING SEX IN ANY OF THESE OPPORTUNITIES?"
CLICK

Then he did too because seriously, who the hell gets a magazine like *Poultry World* aside from the guy upstairs designing chicken torture devices who also happens to make 36 times our combined salaries?

Also? I'm just now realizing I went to college for the wrong thing.

After a few moments, I left the room to find Bob, another of our engineers (actual engineer) who had the same sense of humor I did and was in on the whole joke. I couldn't keep it to myself and knew Bob was the perfect candidate to tell.

Me: "OHMYGOD Jim just got the first magazine."

Bob: "NO!"

Me: "Yes!"

Oh yes.

And the magazines kept coming.

After that first day, it was a constant deluge of chicken magazines arriving in Jim's inbox. ***Chicken Weekly***. ***Chicken Monthly***. ***Chickens Chickens Chickens***.

Then the phone calls began. And they always started the same – with Julie beeping Jim's phone.

> **Julie:** "Jim? You have a phone call."

> **Jim:** "Okay. Thanks."

Then, with my back turned and my head down, I would get Jim's side of the call. Which always went something like this:

> **Jim:** "Hi. Yes. This is Jim. Who? From where? Chicken what? Okay. I don't know ... no. No I don't manufact ... No. I don't do anything with chickens. No I'm not interested. No thank you. NO THANK YOU."

click

And there I sat, head down, laughing so hard I couldn't breathe, trying to keep from gasping that *laugh-gasp* thing you do when you're trying to be quiet, but you're laughing so hard inside that the inhale makes you go, "HEEEEEE."

That? That's what I was doing.

After every phone call or magazine delivery, I ran and told Bob, and we laughed and laughed and laughed until ... one day ...

Yes, this is Jim. You're from Poultry who? What? No. No I didn't..no. NO. STOP CALLING ME.

Jim

me →

Artist's rendition of what it was like when the phone rang for Jim.

> **Julie:** "Jim. You have a phone call."

> **Jim:** "Who is it?"

Julie: "He says he's Inspector Richards from the Postmaster General."

Jim: "Okay. Thanks."

I perked my head up.

Um.

Uh-oh.

Me: "Who?"

Jim: "You know these magazines and calls I keep getting? One of the places told me that they got it from a magazine subscription card. So I called the Post Office to find out what could be done and they want to investigate because it's considered mail fraud."

Me: "Oh."

Anna Kournikova checking me out

me

Artist's rendition of "DID YOU SAY 'MAIL FRAUD'?!?!?!?"

My heart raced. Mail fraud? I just wanted to send him three years of *Pluckers Digest*! I jumped from my seat and ran to Bob.

Me: "BOB. OHMYGODOHMYGOD."

I spilled everything I'd just heard from Jim.

Bob: "Well. Just let it play out. See what happens."

So I casually strolled back into the office like I'd just gone to the bathroom, and Jim was on the phone writing things down saying, "Uh-huh. Uh-huh. Yep. I know it's mail fraud. Who? Okay. Okay I'll call him right now."

Jim hung up the phone and was PISSED.

Me: "What's wrong?"

Jim: "They want me to drive to Boston. One of the companies sent in the subscription card so they want me to see if I recognize the handwriting. I have to call this "Detective Rogers" guy from the FBI right now because it's also a felony. I don't have TIME FOR THIS BULLSHIT."

Me: "Man. That sucks."

For me. That sucks for me SO BAD.

In full panic mode, I ran to Bob again.

Me: "BOB OHMYGOD JIM HAS TO GO THE FBI AND I'M GOING TO GO TO JAIL BECAUSE IT'S A GODDAMN FELONY HOLY SHIT I DON'T WANT TO BE RAPED, BOB, I HAVE SUCH A CUTE LITTLE BUM WHAT DO I DO?!"

Bob: "Well ... maybe go upstairs and talk to George. Tell him everything. We have corporate lawyers and stuff."

I looked at Bob. I think. I'm not sure. I was woozy since all my blood was tightening around my sphincter trying to keep me from CRAPPING MY PANTS.

Me: "Okay. Oh my God. Oh my God, okay."

So I turned and walked upstairs like Sean Penn in "Dead Man Walking," but without Susan Sarandon's googly eyes staring back at me.

Side Note: I think Susan Sarandon is weird-looking. I know people think she's hot, but I don't see it. No? Just me? Where was I?

Oh. Penance. It was time to fess up.

So I stepped into George's office and there was Jim, already talking to George.

Me: "What's up?"

Jim: "Just telling George I have to head to Boston. I can't believe this."

Tick. Tock. Tick ... tock ... it was time. It was time to tell.

Me: "Um ... Jim ... I ... I ..."

I told him everything. I told him about the magazine cards and the phone calls and how Bob told me I should fess up, and most of all, I told him, "I DON'T WANT TO GO TO JAIL AND BE RAPED, JIM! I DON'T WANT TO BE RAPED!"

I turned around and showed Jim my cute little bum. I saw the concern in his gaze about my prison fate because I do, in fact, have a pretty nice ass.

I am buying SO MUCH OF THIS.

Jim: "Are you fucking kidding me?"

Me: "No. I'm not. I'm so sorry."

Jim: "Well. Let me call this FBI guy and see what he says."

Jim took the index card out of his pocket and started dialing. George was still sitting at his desk and Bob had come into the room at this point. I was insane with fear.

Jim: "Hi. Detective Rogers, please." There was a pause. "Hi, Detective. It's Jim. Well ... we found out who did it, so I don't know if you still need me to come down. It's a co-worker of mine, and it was just a joke. I know. I know it's still a felony. I understand 5-10 years, sir."

Oh, look! I think I'm fainting! Are those daisies!?

Jim: "Actually, yes. The person is right here. Yes, sir."

holds phone out

Jim: "He wants to talk to you."

I gulped. I'm not sure what I was gulping because I'm pretty positive I had no spit – a heart rate of 373 beats-per-minute can do that to you. I reached out and grabbed the phone. My eyes welled.

Me: "Hello."

Julie: "HI RODNEY!"

Julie? Front-desk Julie?

Julie: "GOTCHA!"

blink

blink blink

What?

I dropped the phone. Everyone in the room burst out laughing.

Jim: "BAM!"

One of the subscription cards I filled out was returned in the mail. Julie, our receptionist *whom Jim was dating at the time* handed it to Jim, who recognized my handwriting and, well ...

... the greatest revenge practical joke in the history of my practical jokes was perpetrated.

And that? That is why I don't do practical jokes much anymore.

That said, I'm tearing these pages out of every copy of this book in my house. My daughter just received her first "Sheep!" magazine and my son's inaugural issue of "Poultry International" should be arriving any day now.

Like I said, I don't do practical jokes much anymore. Unless they're on my kids who aren't smart enough for retaliation like that.

Yet.

"TAKEN" - A SHADY HOSTAGE STORY

Situation Day 1

Sometimes something catches your attention that is so absurd you have no choice but to make fun of it. For example, take the anomaly of Carrot Top, or anything to do with Paris Hilton, or Winona Ryder's penchant for stealing, or maybe Miley Cyrus and her "Wrecking Ball" video. Great. Now I'm wishing Paris Hilton would show up drunk at Carrot Top's house and steal something with the aid of Winona Ryder while riding Miley Cyrus' wrecking ball.

I bet Carrot Top is now wishing the exact. Same. Thing.

Such an opportunity appeared to me one day as I was going down to the gym at work. I noticed *MISSING* posters taped to the walls. They were in our recreation room, the locker room, hallways, ladies bathroom ...

I mean ... um ... they were PROBABLY in the ladies bathroom.

whistles and walks away

My point is, those *MISSING* posters were hung up **everywhere.**

As I wandered over to one of them, I wondered to myself what this person had lost. What could have gone missing that they felt compelled to go to such great lengths in plastering posters all over work?

Missing child?

Lost dog?

Tara Reid's virginity?

Although my suspicion was that the lost dog had something to do with Tara Reid's virginity. Maybe the missing child was Tara Reid who grew up and lost her virginity to the dog and wow this story just got really sad and gross.

What could be missing? As I approached the sign and looked it over, I discovered what was so priceless to this person.

Um. Dude. Really? Sunglasses?

I mean, those posters were **everywhere.** I honestly don't think that much work went into finding the Lindbergh baby. Fifty extra points to you if you understand the Lindbergh baby reference. A hundred demerit points to you for being so old. So, so old.

There were fifteen **MISSING** posters strewn about the office. All for a stupid pair of sunglasses. I fully expected to order a milk in the cafeteria and see a picture of the sunglasses on the side.

LAST SEEN: March 15, 2010

AGE AT TIME OF DISAPPEARANCE: ?!?!?!

DATE OF BIRTH: no idea

GENDER: um..male..?

HEIGHT: 1-1/2 inches

WEIGHT: couple of ounces

HAIR: might be some stuck, yes

EYES: currently UNSHADED

RACE: I don't like to run

LAST SEEN WEARING:
I don't know what the glasses were wearing. Maybe other sunglasses cuz it was sunny

I mean ... what asshole does this?

So, I did what any normal person would do.

I faked a ransom note for them.

Mr

I have your Ray Bans

Dont wurry   they r safe   for now

If u ever want To see them again   you will leave fOuR
MLLION DOLLARS in unmarked bills near the vending
machines today at FIVE pm SHARP.

NO COPS

I will B watching u   If I see any fuzz u will never see
your Ray Bans again and need to wear cheap shades from
Target HAHAHA

I m serius

five pm fOuR million dollars

every minute u are late I put a tiny scratch in a lens

Red Squirrel X

Please note that I had no intention of hanging around work until five to see if he would actually bring four million dollars. Technically I'm on salary, and anything past noon is considered a full day, so staying as late as 5 pm for any reason is just plain stupid.

I hung it the note next to one of the *'Missing'* posters:

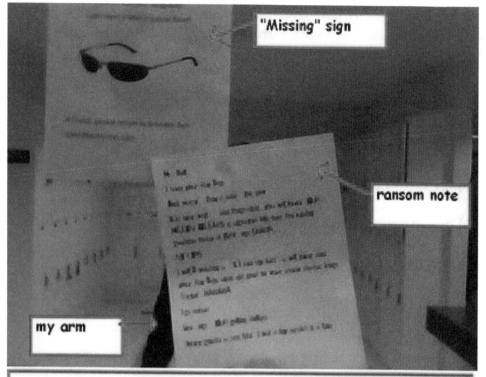

"Missing" sign

ransom note

my arm

The proof is in the pudding. That sounds like horrible pudding.

Of course I didn't actually have his sunglasses, but if this guy had four million bucks, I'd totally be willing to go buy a pair and swap with him. Hell, he already gave me a picture of what they looked like.

It was worth a shot.

Situation Day 2

I walked into the locker room to find some guy angrily removing my ransom note. What in the sweet name of Cheez-Its was going on?

Me: "Those your missing sunglasses?"

Guy: "Yeah. Someone thinks it's a joke. Those glasses cost me a fucking fortune."

Me: "Maybe you should give the guy what he wants. He sounds c-r-a-z-y."

I made the twirly crazy sign and the guy frowned at me, crumpled up the ransom note, and threw it in the trash.

Not only did the guy have complete disregard for me but also for the well-being of his Ray Bans. As such, I decided to play on his sense of compassion for his stupid sunglasses.

RANSOM NOTE #2:

M- ████

You did not leave four million dollars as instructed

Your precius Ray Bans now have a tiny nick in one of

the lenses and theyre all smudgy now

You brought this on yourself

To show u Im willing to comepromize I will change my

reQuest to TWO MILLION dollars to be left near the

vending machines That s a FIFTY PERCENT SAVINGS

for you

NO COPS again please Thanks in advance

If u don t think Im serius look at the attached photo

HAHAHAHA sunglasses DO cry HAHAHAHA

Red SQuirrel X

Then I attached this picture with a piece of tape:

And I hung it up next to his original *MISSING* note just like before:

The next day, both notes were gone. As were all the **MISSING** flyers strewn about the building.

So I didn't get my four million – or even two million – but having this kind of fun at some idiot's expense over a pair of sunglasses is something I'd do over and over again.

For, like, one million bucks. But that's my final offer.

BRAIN NUGGET

IT'S IMPORTANT TO ENCOURAGE
CHILDREN TO DO SOMETHING THEY
NORMALLY WOULDN'T TRY.
LIKE BE QUIET OR GO AWAY.

BRAIN NUGGET

EXCITED TO COACH SOCCER
PRACTICE TONIGHT BECAUSE I
ALWAYS LOVE ENDING A DAY
BY SCREAMING AT
OTHER PEOPLE'S CHILDREN .

YOUR CALL IS VERY IMPORTANT TO US ...
UNLESS YOU HAVE AN ACCENT

A lot of people ask me what I actually do for work. Sadly, my boss is also one of these people.

As you've previously read, you know that I hold a degree in Architectural Engineering. It's not mine, I'm just holding it. IT BELONGS TO A FRIEND, MOM. IT'S NOT MINE, I SWEAR I'M JUST HOLDING IT FOR HIM.

Gah. Sorry. Total digression there.

I never became a full-fledged architect, though, because designing things that aren't supposed to fall down is way more work than it sounds like. Once upon a time I actually knew the tensile strength of steel and the bending properties of concrete, and honestly, I've fallen asleep twice just writing that.

Also, I would have had to do an internship for two years, and by the time I graduated I had amassed $20k worth of credit card bills. In my defense, that money was primarily spent trying to make my 1970 muscle car stupid fast so I could try to get laid at the beach. Even budding architects have penises, people.

Except lady architects. They probably don't have penises. Then again, I wouldn't know because I'd be bored to death from them talking about the tensile strength of steel, thus forgetting about wanting to have sex with them altogether and falling asleep. That's when they'd attack my unconscious body with their lady architect penises. All of this is conjecture, mind you, but the moral of the story is: "If you're out on a date with a lady architect, put on your **no-means-no** underwear." Which means they have permanent skid marks.

Long story short, I didn't become an architect. Instead, I branched into the wonderfully well-paying world of computer technology.

Although I don't do it any more, I was a Technical Support Representative in the Internet Security industry for many years. When you don't like people in general, Technical Support is probably not the best career choice.

The prospect of someone like me working in tech support also explains why your computer got hacked last week and 165 of your Facebook friends clicked on links they thought YOU sent them about black market Viagra, and now they hate you. Except that guy Steve who bought two boxes of them. He's pretty happy with his black market stiffy and getting laid. Maybe even by a lady architect. No one knows but Steve.

No one knows but Steve.

I've since moved on from the role of Tech Support, but every once in a while I still have to call someone because I've run into something that I can't solve myself. Personally, I disdain having to call Tech Support because it always goes like this:

Me: "Yeah, hi. I can't get to the Internet."

Support: "Well that sounds just awful. I'm so sorry. Is your computer actually on?"

Me: "Um. Yeah. Listen, I've been in IT for 15 years, so I think we can skip right to stuff like a DNS issue or a problem with an upstream router."

Support: "I'm sorry, sir. We have a checklist to go through so can you just tell me 'yes' or 'no?' Is your computer actually on?"

Me: "ARE YOU KIDDING ME?! I'm not a moron."

Support: "Sir, I understand your frustration. Is your computer on or not?"

looks down at dark computer

Me: "I'll call you back."

I know a lot of you people out there hate calling Technical Support lines, and as a former Tech Support Rep, I can pretty much assure you that we hate getting your calls just as much. Some quick translations for you:

"How can I help you?" = *"I don't want to help you."*

"Please hold." = *"I hope you hang up while I'm off pooping."*

"Try it and call me right back." = *"I'm going home."*

That said, I came up with a flowchart explaining the behind-the-scenes process of what happens at the technical support center when you call, and all we want to do is go back to sitting on the futon in the rec room while discussing World of Warcraft. Enjoy.

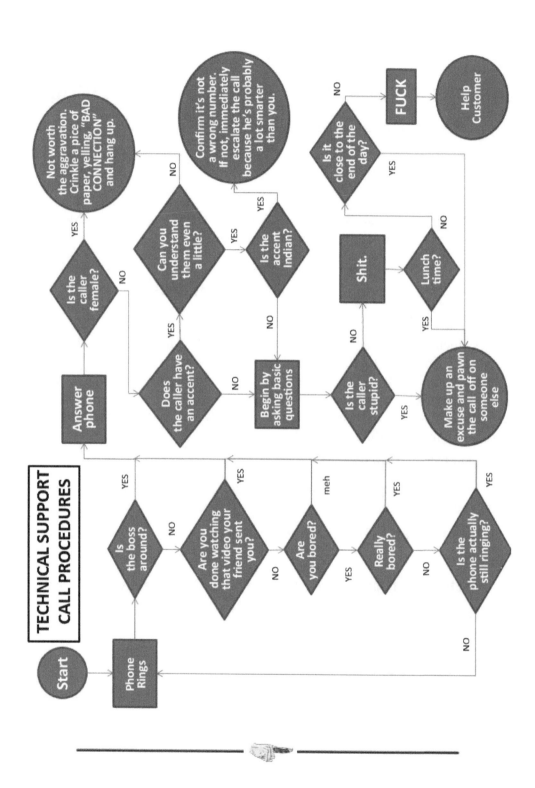

TECHNICAL SUPPORT CALL PROCEDURES

OBJECTS IN YOUR INSTANT MESSENGER WINDOW MAY APPEAR SMALLER THAN THEY ARE

My job in Technical Support required me to use an Instant Message program in order to talk to our cohorts in Oregon.

Oregon State Motto: "Yay trees."

Back then, my company used Yahoo! Instant Messenger as their IM program. Being new to the computer industry at the time, I didn't have a Yahoo account, so I began the arduous task of setting one up. My previous Instant Message program was on my America Online account which I would access by my analog modem I bought at Radio Shack that I drove to in a car powered by my feet while I ate brontosaurus ribs.

I cannot believe I am this old.

As I was signing up, I ran into a major hurdle. Almost all the user names I tried were already gone.

SupportMan - *[That account name has already been taken]*

Dammit.

TechSupportMan - *[That account name has already been taken]*

UGH.

Okay. Time to get creative.

SupportMidget

See? I'm in support, and even though I'm not technically a midget, I'm really short so that would be perfect ...

[That account name has already been taken]

ARE YOU KIDDING ME?!?!?!?

That was when I started getting pissed.

MidgetMan - *[That account name has already been taken]*

OMGOMGOMG I AM GOING TO KILL SOMEONE ... Think. Think. Man ... man of steel ...

MidgetManOfSteel - *[Account created]*

Bam. And thus my user name *midgetmanofsteel* was born. And I carry the moniker to this very day, although now I believe I'm the only person left using Yahoo mail – but if you think I'm going through this crap again with Gmail, you are sadly mistaken.

So time went on and I continued to use Instant Messenger every day. It sat right there prominently running on my desktop in the event someone in Oregon had a computer question that needed answering quickly. In turn, I could ask anyone in Oregon things that they specialized in, like what kind of marijuana was the best and how to correctly spell the word "hippie."

One day I was teaching a technology class, sitting at the front of the classroom with my laptop facing me, and suddenly my IM window opened up. The message wasn't from anyone in the building or in Oregon.

It was an IM from someone I had never heard of before.

SomeGirl: *hello?*

Me: *um ... hi?*

SomeGirl: *Saw your profile. How tall are you?*

??? How tall am ... OH. My nickname ... MIDGETManOfSteel.

I'm not a midget. I am a man. I am not a midget man. I am not a man of steel. Midget Steel would be a cool name for a tiny rock band.

Turns out that only 20% of my Instant Messenger name was true. The other 80% made it sound like I was a sexy ripped midget who may or may not play a musical instrument. By choosing this name, I had inadvertently started messing with people in the best possible way.

Me: *um ... what? Who is this?*

SomeGirl: *Like, can I pick you up and toss you around?*

Me: *Mom?*

SomeGirl: *Do you like being tossed around? How tall are you? Do you like being carried around by your women like a backpack?*

At that point a few things were becoming clear to me:

1) I was completely neglecting my class.
2) It was kind of creepy. Although, being carried around like a backpack did sound kind of fun.
3) I was starting to wish I was a midget.

Somegirl: *Hello? Little man? What do you weigh? Do you like being bench pressed?*

Me: *Ooookay. Listen, I'm not an actual midget. I'm 5-foot-3.*

   (... pause ...)

SomeGirl: *Oh.*

   (... pause ...)

   (SomeGirl has signed out)

What. The. Fuck.

That marked the first time I ever realized that chicks dig midgets. I had no idea. I suppose I could have asked my friends in Oregon about this phenomenon, but they were usually pretty baked.

Nothing like that ever happened to me again, but I still have my *MidgetManOfSteel* user name, so I'm hopeful.

Hmmm ... adding to bucket list ... carried around like a backpack ...

WORK IS STARTING TO CRAMP MY LAVISH LIFESTYLE

I often check my work email at night. This is because all slackers know that the real way to feign being a workaholic is to randomly respond to work emails at all hours and make sure you "cc" your boss even if the emails have nothing to do with you or your boss or your actual job.

From:	▦ Facilities	Sent:	Fri 2/25/2011 9:33 PM
To:	▦ Entire Company		
Cc:			
Subject:	Parking Lot Maintenance		

perfect!

Please be advised that we will be repainting the parking spot lines on Saturday, February 26th. If you're planning on being in the office that day, you will need to park on the side of the building instead of the rear lot.

If you get this email...

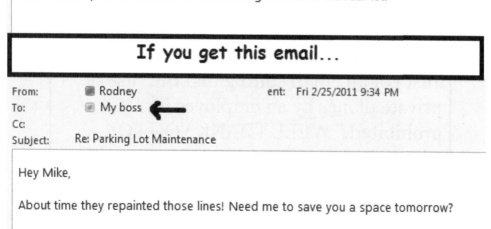

From:	▦ Rodney	ent:	Fri 2/25/2011 9:34 PM
To:	▦ My boss		
Cc:			
Subject:	Re: Parking Lot Maintenance		

Hey Mike,

About time they repainted those lines! Need me to save you a space tomorrow?

...Send out this.

Just a helpful tip for keeping you gainfully employed if you have the work ethic of a corn kernel.

Like me.

You're welcome.

So one day at work, this email arrived in my inbox:

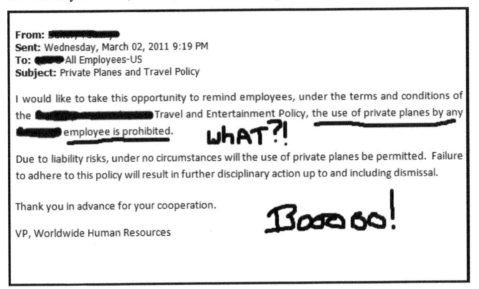

From: ▓▓▓▓▓▓▓
Sent: Wednesday, March 02, 2011 9:19 PM
To: ▓▓▓All Employees-US
Subject: Private Planes and Travel Policy

I would like to take this opportunity to remind employees, under the terms and conditions of the ▓▓▓▓▓▓▓▓▓▓Travel and Entertainment Policy, the use of private planes by any ▓▓▓▓▓ employee is prohibited. *WhAT?!*

Due to liability risks, under no circumstances will the use of private planes be permitted. Failure to adhere to this policy will result in further disciplinary action up to and including dismissal.

Thank you in advance for your cooperation. *Boooo!*

VP, Worldwide Human Resources

WHAT?!?!? NO PRIVATE PLANES?!?!?!

This injustice will not stand. In my furor, I Tweeted:

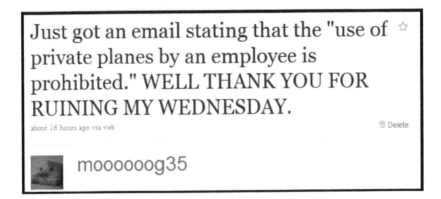

Just got an email stating that the "use of private planes by an employee is prohibited." WELL THANK YOU FOR RUINING MY WEDNESDAY.

about 16 hours ago via web — Delete

mooooog35

Then, remembering my golden *"feign you're a workaholic"* rule, I sent out this email to my boss:

> **From:** Lacroix, Rodney
> **Sent:** Wednesday, March 02, 2011 9:35 PM
> **To:** ▓▓▓▓▓ Michael
> **Subject:** FW: Private Planes and Travel Policy
>
>
> Well, if I have to fly regular airlines, Mike, I guess I'm gonna be a little late tomorrow.

That says *"Hey, boss. I'm checking my email way later than I should be, just in case someone is trying to get hold of me for work-related crap, but here is a funny reply that will endear you to me even more **and** also gives me an excuse to come in later than usual tomorrow."*

The more you know.

A few minutes later I received this from my boss:

> **From:** ▓▓▓▓▓ Michael
> **Sent:** Wednesday, March 02, 2011 9:39 PM
> **To:** Lacroix, Rodney
> **Subject:** RE: Private Planes and Travel Policy
>
>
> I'm trying to figure out what I'm going to do with my new Cessna if I'm not allowed to fly it...

That actually made me laugh.

And that, my fine readers, is *"How to Bullshit Your Way Through Gainful Employment 101."*

Maybe I should stop giving this advice away for free. I'd probably be able to buy my own private plane from all the cash I'd get from selling my tips.

Too bad I won't be able fly the damn thing to work.

CHIQUITA KNOWS ALL ...

If you skip this story you will regret it for the rest of your life. Trust me on this one as I am about to impart on you some wisdom that will open new doors in your life.

If there's even a tiny bit of you that likes to mess around with people, this chapter will be like a Tony Robbins seminar but with less personal motivation and more screwing with others. I'm talking about the trick of scoring words into banana peels. Yes, you read that right: This is about writing on bananas.

All you have to do to make this work is take a toothpick or tip of a sharp knife, and write some stuff on a new or unripe banana. You should also probably be mentally unstable.

What you write on the banana is up to you, BUT through some sort of hokus-pokus – and probably something to do with science – the words you write will magically appear on the fruit days later.

One morning I woke up in my fiancée's house and was perusing around her kitchen when, amidst the empty vodka bottles, I spied a bunch of bananas.

This showed up on her Facebook page two days later (opposite page).

I like how Rosanne completely ignores the creepy writing on the banana and, instead, recommends a recipe. Way to focus there, Rosanne.

Of course, I fessed up because I enjoy having sex sometimes, and I don't need my fiancée trying to ward off evil banana spirits 24 hours a day while I sit in the corner by myself playing with my own banana.

Priorities, yo.

One day, while wandering around aimlessly at work and randomly going through cubicle drawers, I realized that a lot of people ate bananas. People brought them in and – because bananas are fine sitting around for a while – left them sitting naked and alone, on their desks.

That *ding* sound you just heard was the light bulb on top of my head.

Kerredith ▓▓▓▓▓
Just found this in my bunch of bananas.... Can you say
FREAKED OUT?!?!?!?!

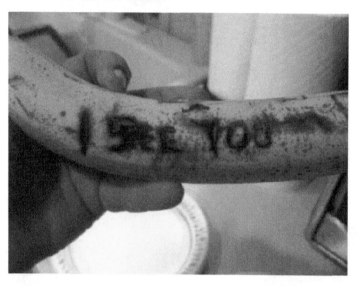

Tracey H▓▓▓▓▓▓▓▓▓▓▓▓i LMAO!!!!
August 3 at 7:20pm · Like

Kerredith ▓▓▓▓▓ I think I need to bury it in the
back yard and do some sort of ritual!!! Lol
August 3 at 8:04pm · Like

Patti ▓▓▓▓▓ Bring it back to the store, you will
get a whole bunch free, I would not eat it
though.....
August 3 at 8:05pm · Like

Dana B▓▓▓▓ That;s wicked creepy....I wouldn't
even eat it..lol
August 3 at 7:23pm · Like

Rosanne ▓▓▓▓▓▓ it is very ripe. you should
make banana bread
August 3 at 7:23pm · Like · 👍 1 person

Tracy ▓▓▓▓▓▓▓▓▓ Be thankful it doesnt say
I SEE DEAD PEOPLE. Just trying to make lemon
drops here........
August 3 at 7:29pm · Like

So when I see an empty cube or have a few extra minutes to root around in
someone's lunchbox in the fridge, I take it upon myself to do stuff like this if I
spy an orphaned banana:

I like coming up with new combinations of banana writing. Here are some helpful selections if you would like to try making ghostly bananas too:

"U LOOK NICE TODAY"

"SPIDERS INSIDE"

"UR FIRED"

"UR ADOPTED"

"I NAILED UR WIFE"

"I WAS IN A BUTT"

"WHORE"

Of course, it all depends on your audience. I highly suggest using the "I nailed your wife" or "whore" in situations outside the workplace, like at church suppers. BONUS: If you're really nailing someone's wife, you can probably use both of those sayings in one bunch of bananas. Consolidation is key.

I would definitely avoid using the above sayings on work bananas unless you know you're already getting fired or quitting. Then, by all means, write all of these on the bananas of the Human Resources Group.

Speaking of work:

The latter banana was actually a guy's in my own workgroup. I'm a repeat offender with his bananas *(As is Julia in payroll ... Yes, we all know, Tim)* and once wrote *"DIE!! 666"* on his banana with an upside-down pentagram.

Sometimes I get too excited when holding a banana and a thumbtack.

I was going to take a picture of the Satanic death-wish banana, but when I went back to do it, my coworker **WAS SHOWING THE BANANA TO MY BOSS.** As such, I felt it was best to admit nothing and run away to live another day as the Banana Ghost Writer.

throws smoke bomb and disappears

Ahh ... the crap I do instead of working ...

We R Watching.

BRAIN NUGGET

I JUST ATE HALF OF THE STICKER
ON MY APPLE IN CASE YOU WERE
WONDERING WHAT KIND OF
PERSON IS IN CHARGE OF YOUR
SOFTWARE QUALITY CONTROL.

ELVIS HAS LEFT THE BUILDING

Once upon a time, I came really close to getting laid.

Off.

Laid off.

When you're me, you take what you can get and call it *"action."*

I cry sometimes.

You say "unemployment" i say "funemployment"

Shortly after starting my current job, a rumor began circulating that layoffs were imminent.

I had only been there eight months at the time, and was pretty much spending the days writing my blog and pretending to be busy as best as I knew how.

If you haven't done it, I must tell you that pretending to work is almost as exhausting as doing the actual work itself. You have to always look concerned about something and swear under your breath whenever your boss is nearby.

As long as your boss sees that you're frustrated and connected 24x7 and doing SOMETHING, you've won half the battle.

Me: "Hey. Did you get the email I sent out last night?"

Boss: "Yes. I'm very excited about the new season of American Idol, too, Rod. So, how's that project I put you on coming along?"

Me (under my breath): "I'M SO FRUSTRATED!"

throws laptop

But you can only pretend to work for so long before someone decides that they need to take a closer look at your actual worth. I assume that my bosses calculate my return on investment by some sort of equation that involves dividing by zero. As such, I was completely expecting this type of meeting to happen as the layoffs neared:

Boss: "Well ... we reviewed your statistics, Rod. According to IT, it appears that although you were in the lab working 20% of the time, the rest of your day is spent Googling stuff like 'ugly penis chickens.'"

Me: "Wow ... 20%?! I had no idea I was working that much."

fist pump

Then I would leave early.

Back to the layoff day ... I had it confirmed that indeed, on that **very** day, there was supposed to be a layoff announcement.

People were nervous. Tensions were high. Bowels were constricted.

As was my normal custom, I spent half my day in the bathroom because when I get nervous, I fart. I'd like to know why that is and – more important – if I'm the only one who does it.

I honestly cannot be the only person who gets nervous farts.

114

Perhaps there is a group that goes by "Nervous Farters Anonymous" (NERFA) and they have the shortest meetings ever because everyone is freaking out when they get there and they're tooting all over the place creating an issue with air quality forcing everyone to leave.

Also, smoking would not allowed in the building for obvious reasons.

So I was getting coffee when I bumped into Iain, a friend of mine from high school who also worked at the company.

The #1 Google Image result for 'ugly penis chickens.'

Yes. I'm very disappointed too.

> **Me:** "You ready for the layoffs?"
>
> **Iain:** "I heard. Ugh. I'm so nervous.
>
> **Me:** "Me too. VERY nervous. That being said, you might want to stand way over there."
>
> **Iain:** "Why?"
>
> **Me:** "No reason. ANYWAY, I'm the last to be hired in my group. So it will be me let go if it's anyone."
>
> **Iain:** "Same here. I'm the last one in."
>
> ***light bulb***
>
> **Me:** "We should email each other throughout the morning just to make sure that our email is still working. Having your email shut off is the harbinger of doom."

Just for the record, I did **NOT** say *"harbinger of doom."*

I hadn't had my first cup of coffee yet so it probably sounded more like:

Me: "No email ... bad for man ... make man be sad!"

No coffee breeds bad decisions.
Just ask a non-caffeinated Hugh Grant.

BRAIN NUGGET

I HAD A GIANT BURRITO
LAST NIGHT AND, WELL,
LET'S JUST SAY I'VE STARTED
MARKING THE DAYS IN
THIS STALL WITH CHALK.

So we made a pact to email each other every so often, just to make sure we still existed in the company's address book.

Because, you know, this is the kind of stuff I do.

At 9:04 AM, I sent Iain this email on the next page:

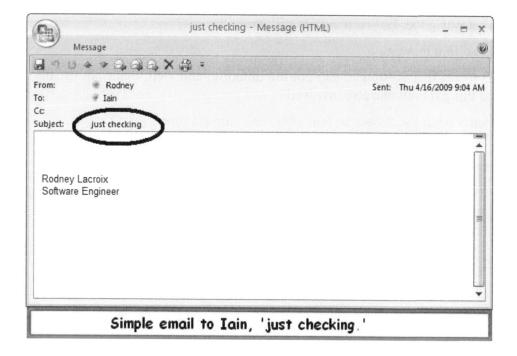

Simple email to Iain, 'just checking.'

About 20 minutes later ... Iain responds:

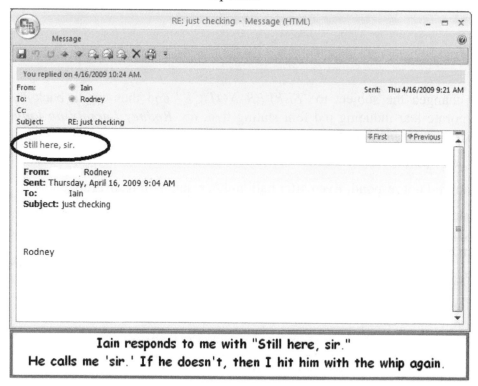

Iain responds to me with "Still here, sir."
He calls me 'sir.' If he doesn't, then I hit him with the whip again.

That was good. Both our emails still worked.

Or so Iain thought.

You see, that 20-minute gap got me thinking, and well, that's not usually a good thing for anyone else involved.

Here's what I sent back to Iain after receiving his reply:

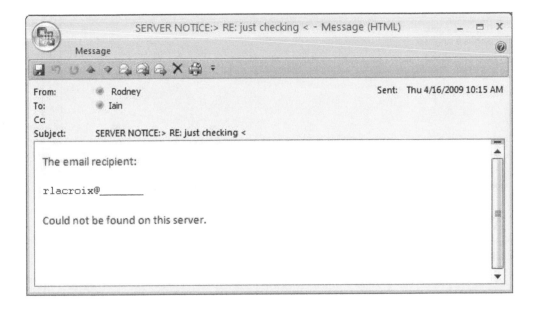

I changed the subject to *"SERVER NOTICE"* and then wrote back in a Corporate fear-inducing red font stating that, no, **Rodney Lacroix no longer existed in the email system**.

Then I sent it.

Iain did not respond. Even after half an hour, Iain still hadn't replied.

Instead, he came upstairs to try to find me but – alas – he did **not** find me because remember that *"spending half my day in the bathroom"* reference from earlier in this story?

Yeah. Oh yeah.

That being said, I should probably go see a doctor.

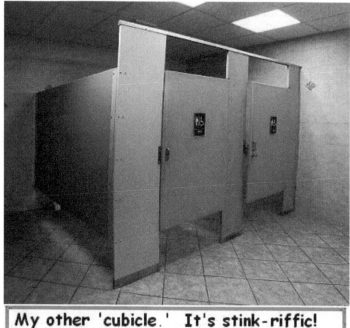

My other 'cubicle.' It's stink-riffic!

Luckily, the IT department can't track me in the bathroom.

So, Iain, after receiving an "undeliverable" email and being unable to find me, thought I'd been laid off. And because of our earlier conversation about being the last one hired, he was pretty positive he'd be the next one to go.

This was confirmed when I headed over to the printer and found Iain's resume sitting in the printer tray.

Aw, crap.

Sometimes, torturing someone works out better than you initially planned. It is for this very reason that if anyone ever actually goes postal at my place of employment, my cubicle will be the gunman's first stop.

In fact, it will probably be his only stop. Now that I'm thinking about it, I should probably update my beneficiaries for my "Death or Dismemberment" insurance.

I picked up Iain's resume off the printer tray. Although this gag worked beyond my wildest dreams, I AM human and humans have feelings. My therapist tries to tell me this all the time while I stare back blankly, reply "beep bop boop," and then do a rendition of my legendary robot dance.

One of these human feelings is supposed to be "compassion." Normally, I put the "ass" in "compassion," but after an hour of letting Iain sweat, I decided it was time to ease his mind.

Resume in hand, I walked to Iain's cube. He was on the phone, one hand running through his hair, his face scrunched like he was holding in a fart, saying:

> **Iain:** "I don't know, honey. It's been quiet. Nobody's even ... is your uncle still hiring?
>
> **Me:** "I think this is yours."

I tossed his resume onto his desk as he looked up.

Iain's shoulders slumped and he breathed out. "You bastard," he said, shaking his head and lowering the phone. "Nicely done."

"Thank you," I replied. Then I backed away while doing my robot dance because it really is quite remarkable.

Iain and I still work together at the same company. But there's a new guy in my group now, so I have that "undeliverable" email ready to go at a moment's notice.

Beep bop boop.

Brain Nugget

The only thing worse than a really cold toilet seat is a really warm one.

And now for something completely different (the Draw Something files)

Ugh. I can hear it now:

> "Hey, Rod. I thought this book was supposed to be about you messing with people. WTF?"

> "Drawings?! What do these pictures have to do with the theme of this book?"

> "How do you keep yourself so fit and attractive? Also, your penis is huge and you have great stamina."

Ugh. If I had a nickel ...

This is the third chapter of this book and has pretty much zilch to do with the actual theme of the book except the fact that my publisher thinks it will help sell more of them.

I can't argue with that kind of sound logic. Spock would say, "Well, he's got a point, Captain," and then I'd concur just like Kirk and head off to bang a hot yeoman in a miniskirt.

Mmmm. Yeoman.

To address the other questions about the "why" of these pictures, the best answer is that the Draw Something section of my first book was so immensely popular that my publisher and I felt we HAD to include some more examples in this book.

If you're unfamiliar with the game, it's a pretty simple concept: you are given a word that you must draw, and your opponent has to guess it. It's kind of like "Pictionary," but without a timer or rules or the need for any real talent. You will see this shortly.

Also important to know is that for the person doing the guessing, the picture is slowly "drawn on the screen" exactly as the artist originally sketched it, like watching a stop-animation sequence.

So with the popularity of these pictures in mind, we decided to temporarily break away from the flow of the book (assuming there's an actual flow) and throw caution to the wind.

"Caution" was the name of my neighbor's cat.

Related: Cats can't fly and the "always landing on the feet" thing is not 100% accurate.

Also related: My neighbor really misses Caution a lot.

Plus, the addition of these pictures gives you, the reader, a well-deserved break from all my run-on sentences and terrible grammar the publisher will inevitably miss.

They're colorful and pretty, and the more pictures I put in here, the less I have to write. There are probably more reasons to include these, but the **more books sold + less writing** is a combination that's proved hard for me to ignore.

I should probably use the profits from the extra book sales to get my neighbor a new cat.

BRAIN NUGGET

I'VE BEEN USING MY CHIN-UP
BAR REGULARLY. I'VE WORKED
UP TO HANGING FIVE SHIRTS AND
A PAIR OF PANTS ON IT.

Ah.

What better way to start off my Draw Something section than with someone in a latex outfit being forced to lick someone's foot?

Right. I can't think of one, either.

This drawing would also be valid if I had to illustrate "Typical Tuesday Night at Rodney's House."

Everyone under 40 will probably need to Google this.

True story:
In 1987 I was working for a firm that was changing healthcare plans.

The new provider was giving a presentation and said: "..and we also include well-baby care."

To which I replied: "I bet Baby Jessica's parents wish they had that."

Then everyone went:
O_O

At this point I've drawn a bondage / latex scene, a comic recreation of a tragic event where a baby fell into a well, and now an old guy shitting in an adult undergarment.

Typical Tuesday, really.

On a side note, I kind of can't wait for the day when I can just be wandering around a Dollar Store, stop, crap my pants, and then go over and buy a pack of Twizzlers.

My bucket list is pretty terrible.

This is actually a terrifying memory from one time when I ate some bad mushrooms.

The difference here is that I decided to draw what it would look like from the policeman's perspective, and not from the point of view of the pickle who is actually driving the burger or his passenger made of flaming oatmeal.

I decided to go the 'family friendly' route here because sometimes I forget who I'm drawing for and send this stuff to my kids by accident.

The other option included a pretty hot scene from Caligula, and really, no one wants to have to explain THAT to their children. Again.

This is one of those cases where everyone who gets the word "Stoner" probably draws some guy smoking a joint.

I ended up going the "Puritan adulteress being murdered" route as it seemed the logical alternative.

Please notice the intricate details on the thatched roofs. Although, I'm pretty sure they didn't have concrete block walls back then.

This also disproves the theory that Puritan blondes had more fun.

I used to like the teacup ride at amusement parks. That is until I hit age thirty when everything that spins started making me throw up.

This phenomenon also includes my steering wheel, which explains my high car insurance rates and multiple vehicular homicide convictions.

Ah.

"The Stranger."

If you were previously unfamiliar with this masturbatory term, this should explain it to you. The world is now your oyster. Go prosper with this new knowledge. You might want to avoid some churches.

What isn't clear here is who this guy is talking to or why he has such a huge headboard for what is obviously a twin bed. I like to keep 'em guessing.

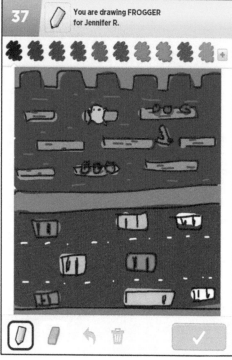

Here we have a prime example of how I layer my drawings.

1. Draw a blue sky background.
2. Draw in the buildings and pavement.
3. Draw a head-on automobile collision between two Phillips head screws, ignoring the fact that (a) they are gigantic, (b) screws don't have arms, and (c) screws can't drive cars or speak
4. Add details like wheel nuts on the cars and the screws flipping each other off.
5. Add foreground details like sidewalk and stop light.

Yep.

That's a turd.

Sure, I could have – you know – just drawn a tooth here. But sometimes the need to piss off an entire culture of people is SO STRONG that I have to go for it.

Part of going for it assumes that the people who are going to be offended (i.e., in this case, NASCAR fans and people who live in Alabama) don't buy books, so I think I'm pretty safe on this one.

Hey Rod, while you're at it, why don't you completely offend Cubans?

I can only imagine this is what my editor was thinking when he put BOTH the 'tooth' drawing and 'Cuba' on the same page. Now when the Cuban refugees land and see my book, they can hook up with the NASCAR fans as they all head north to kill me to death. My editor can be an ASSHOLE.

In my defense, you totally would have guessed Cuba here if I sent this to you, too, so you are all now accomplices. I'll let the Alabamans and Cubans know when they get here.

So now you know what the "Reverse Cowgirl" position is as well as "The Stranger" masturbation technique.

I'm like Dr. Ruth but without the accent and affinity for sticking cucumbers in my hoo-ha. Mainly because I don't have a hoo-ha. But if I did, I still don't know that I'd put a cucumber in there. Seems like a waste of money with cukes being $1.26/pound as of this writing.

I forgot where I was going with this.

This one could have gone a couple of ways, but I decided to go with Charlie and his grandpa standing at the gates of the Willy Wonka chocolate factory.

The other option was showing everyone licking wallpaper, but I got distracted with the resulting images I found Googling 'licking wallpaper' for references to use.

Two hours and fifteen tissues later, I decided to draw this. Fish or cut bait, people. Fish or cut bait.

This is one of those where the drawing unfolded for the person like this:

Pink. Blue. Okay ... so it's a pink wall and a blue floor. What's he drawing on the ... OH ... okay ... it's a painting on the wall. Hmm. Art? Painting? No ... that's not it. OH. He's drawing a person. It's an angry mad woman. Okay. Wait. Here's another person lying down. Sprawled. The other person is sprawled on the floor. Blood and X-eyes. The other person is dead. WTF IS HE DRAWING? Oh. Okay. Scissors.

And that's what it's like to play Draw Something with me.

With this drawing, I felt the need to unveil the horror that a fish would experience while watching her eggs being eaten by someone.

I don't know why I felt this need. I'm assuming it's because I have some serious issues. But probably not as many issues as someone who would eat the eggs of their pet goldfish.

It's now becoming obvious that I'm not tolerant of a lot of people or cultures.

It's also becoming painfully clear to me that my editor wants me to die at the hands of an international mob.

We are now taking a break from our regularly scheduled offensive Draw Somethings to show you my rendition of 'breath.'

I think we've all experienced a time when our significant other rolls over in the morning and Satan comes out of his or her mouth. In this case, it actually kills the woman.

Please note that this is also the first time I've drawn a brunette woman because my fiancée keeps giving me crap about always drawing blondes. "ANOTHER BLONDE?" she asks. "ANOTHER ONE?!"

So, yes. I drew a brunette. And she's dead now. I hope you're happy, Kerri. I hope you're happy.

It was just a matter of time before Wilbur and Charlotte had a falling out.

This is one of my favorite Draw Somethings.

As soon as I got the word "nun," my mind went to "flying nun" which then turned into "I could either draw Sally Field" or draw "someone trying to make a nun fly by pushing her off of a cliff." Sometimes the choices are obvious.

The fact that there's another nun standing behind them sadly waiting also indicates that this experiment has been going on for a while.

Sometimes I get really sensitive and emotional when creating my Draw Something pictures.

Then there are times like this when I draw a killer whale eating a marine biologist.

We're just going to file this one under the 'self-explanatory' category and call it a day.

I think the only thing out-of-sorts with this one is the surprised look on my face as I'm told I belong in hell. Although my horror may or may not be a result of me realizing that I don't have hands.

"Hmmm. How should I draw, "Dutch?""

Boy in wooden clogs? No.

Two people splitting the bill for a meal? Nah.

The flag of the Netherlands? Pfft.

Guy farting under the blankets and then holding his girlfriend's head under so she is forced to smell it? Yep. I think we have a winner..

In hindsight, I realize that my rendition of "the straw that broke the camel's back" actually looks more like "two StormTroopers on Tatooine arguing over a dead tauntaun with back tumors outside Jabba the Hutt's house."

Po-TA-to, po-TAH-to.

[*You know who you are.*]

It was only a matter of time before Bobby McFerrin made his way into my Draw Something world.

In this case, it just so happened to be in front of a homeless guy who is, quite obviously, sick of Bobby's shit.

136

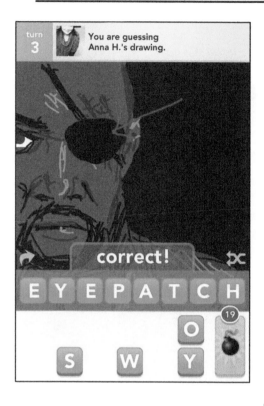

This one is obviously not mine because it is really good, but just goes to show you what something can look like if you don't always have your mind in the gutter. Also, you should probably have some type of artistic talent.

So, in a nutshell, if you can draw and keep your hands out of your own pants then maybe – God willing – you can draw Nick Fury as effing awesome as this.

Draw Something starts out by giving you three word suggestions. You then pick one and draw it.

Or, you read all three of them together. Then you laugh for five minutes straight because you have the mindset of a twelve-year-old, and "Butt Pirate Worship" sounds like the. Best. Porno. Ever.

Considering I drew this on a tiny little iPod with just my fingertip and a prayer, I have to admit that this is a pretty kick-ass rendition of "Saturday Night Fever."

This is also eerily similar to what I look like when I go out on weekends.

And also why no one asks me to go out with them on weekends.

If you haven't already noticed, one of my signature things to do with Draw Something is to punctuate my point with a person swearing.

Yes, I could have easily have gotten the point across with the scale saying "GET OFF, PLEASE!" but I think the reaction of the person on the scale kind of seals the deal.

Plus I have kids, so I'm usually yelling "OH FUDGE" or "WHAT THE CRAP" in my house, and it's kind of cathartic to be able to spell "FUCK YOU" in a picture to relieve the pressure.

I haven't seen this commercial in a while so some of you might be going, "Why are rotting testicles wearing sunglasses singing on a stage here?" To which I reply, "BECAUSE THEY CAN."

Sure, I could have drawn a mythical creature from "Clash of the Titans" but – instead – decided to go with the image of Perseus' mom banging on the bathroom door because he'd been in there for twenty minutes taking a dump.

On a related note, after my kids and I first saw "Clash of the Titans," we referred to pooping as 'releasing the Kracken' for a few months. It was a very funny few months, so I highly suggest doing this in your household if your household is like mine where everyone announces when they're going to take a shit.

I'm looking at this now and wondering when Gabe Kaplan was cast in 'Anchorman.'

If you don't remember who Gabe Kaplan is, think "Welcome Back, Kotter."

If you don't remember "Welcome Back, Kotter," fuck you.

I'm looking at this headboard and wondering if it's the same guy from my 'Stranger' drawing, but now he's bought a bigger bed.

Apparently, buying a bigger bed also means you get to stop masturbating and start having nookie. Also, please note that he just banged a blonde here, so I probably got yelled at by my fiancée again for not making her a brunette.

I love the look on the guys' face, though, like, "Yeah. I'm the shit for going at it for five minutes straight."

I'm so jealous.

This is one of those drawings that only works if the person knows what the hell I'm drawing. In this case, I drew a Dunkin Donuts which is a hugely popular donut franchise that sells little donut balls called 'munchkins.'

The tie-in here is that the guy in the drive-thru is naked and his 'munchkins' are hanging out.

Obviously this doesn't play well if the person on the other side has never heard of Dunkin Donuts. Or munchkins. Or testicles.

Great. Now I want testicle-shaped donuts.

This one is pretty self-explanatory.

I don't know why I put 24x7 service, though.

That sounds frigging exhausting.

Socially Distorted

A brief history lesson:

Once upon a time, God invented Friendster.

Friendster begat MySpace.

MySpace begat Mark Zuckerberg.

Mark Zuckerberg begat Facebook. Unless you talk to the Winklevoss twins. Then THEY begat Facebook but still haven't convinced any judges of this. Plus they actually seem more pompous than Zuckerberg, so I really have no issues here.

Then Facebook begat Twitter.

People Tweeted that Facebook should have a dislike button. Mark Zuckerberg kept begat-ing changes to Facebook that pissed people off like that goddamn timeline and OMG WHAT HAPPENED TO MY NEWS FEED THIS TIME?!!?!?

Jesus wept.

As you have seen in the previous chapters, I enjoy screwing with people. I especially like screwing with people when it means I'm actually screwing and the people are women who are at least a little conscious. Or unconscious. I'm not picky, really.

And now you know why I titled the book the way I did.

But, yeah, I like screwing with people. People I know. People I don't know. People I only know because you might know them even if I only suspect you know them and still can't figure out Facebook's Privacy Settings. Confused people (like yourself, right now). Famous people. Corporations. News personalities. Tall people. Confused tall famous news personalities.

You get the idea.

This tendency to mess around with the sanity of others became infinitely more fun when social media hit the mainstream. Twitter. Facebook. LinkedIn.

Instant Messaging. The world suddenly became my oyster. I realized that by harnessing the power of social media, I could become an asshole on a global scale.

It was a temptation that someone like me found impossible to ignore.

Here, on the following pages, you will see what happens when a desire to brighten someone's day with a laugh meets the need to make someone go, "OH MY GOD, SERIOUSLY?!" meets my Internet access without any firewall filtering.

If there's a bizarre news story happening, or if you post something on Facebook or Twitter, or even if you send me a serious Instant Message, you have a pretty good chance that I'll reply if the window of sarcastic opportunity is open.

I could do this all week. That is, if I didn't rest on the seventh day. I can only beget this crap for so long.

BRAIN NUGGET

"YOU WILL DIE AT 2 AM
AND ANGER EVERY
PERSON AROUND YOU."
- A SMOKE DETECTOR BATTERY
HAVING HIS FORTUNE READ.

BREAKING NEWS AND OTHER FRAGILE ITEMS

I have a confession to make.

I watch the news.

Mainly because the local stations hire hot chicks to do the weather. This tends to be a problem because I end up focusing on their bodies and mannerisms and go daydreaming when they say things like, "there's moisture coming from the South."

Long story short, I haven't actually heard what the weather is supposed to be on any given day for the last five years.

puts on parka in middle of August

My local Fox News station reads viewer Tweets and Facebook posts in relation to stories they are covering. As a result, I've developed a pretty good relationship with a couple of the news anchors and am actually featured on their viewer segments regularly.

They don't pay royalties, so I'm basically doing this for the publicity and the chance that I'll get some sort of Marilyn Monroe-type break, except instead of discovering me looking sexy in a diner, I'll be sitting at home Tweeting something funny about vehicular homicide.

To-MA-to, *to-MAH-to*.

Here are a couple of interactions I've had with the local news stations here in New England. In between the sexy weather segments, of course.

One of my favorite local anchors is a guy named Gene Lavanchy. He's got a great sense of humor, and we often talk on Twitter about things that aren't necessarily related to that day's news stories. You could say we have a bromance, but I think it's less "bromance" and more "news anchor has a creepy stalking viewer guy probably in need of a restraining order."

A good example of this is right here, when I told him I was getting a tattoo of him. In my defense, I actually WAS getting a tattoo, but I'm not one to miss out on a opportunity to have a conversation with a news anchor or celebrity about something stupid.

---

moooooog35 @moooooog35   3h
@fox25gene FYI, I'm getting a tattoo tonight. Just so I'm clear, it's
spelled L-A-V-A-N-C-H-Y, right?
Expand

Gene Lavanchy @fox25gene   2h
@moooooog35 There is a copyright..no tattoos allowed!
Expand

---

moooooog35 @moooooog35   2h
@fox25gene ugh. Fine. But it's a shame. The design had such
great detail on the fire-breathing unicorn and your gladiator outfit.
Expand

Gene Lavanchy @fox25gene   2h
@moooooog35 Maybe we'll go with t-shirts then!
● Hide conversation ← Reply ⤴ Retweet ★ Favorite

7:08 AM - 25 Jul 12 via web · Details

See? T-shirts. Genius. Or maybe "Gene-ius." I'm just glad I got a temporary tattoo because I had no idea there was a copyright infringement there.

Note: Tread carefully with your local news anchors. Not all of them will respond to your antics in kind. Like this other local news station that did a story listing Massachusetts towns having the most births to unmarried mothers under thirty years old.

The station apparently has no sense of humor, but thirteen people reading the post appreciated my take on it:

WCVB Channel 5 Boston · 76,209 like this
21 hours ago ·

Over half the births to women under 30 are to unmarried mothers.

We've prepared a list of the

Massachusetts towns where this is the "new normal."

 Mass. towns with most unmarried mothers
www.wcvb.com

More than half of births to American women under 30 occur outside marriage.
Motherhood without marriage has settled deeply into middle America.

 Rodney Lacroix So basically what you're doing is giving us a list of places where
the women are easy? THANK YOU SO MUCH.
21 hours ago · Like · 👍 13

Best. Road trip. Ever.

Then there are some stories that you just HAVE to comment on.

If you read my first book, you know that I dedicated an entire chapter to my vasectomy. Some people called this a little overkill, where others said it took balls. Tiny little balls. Tiny little balls with incisions in them.

My point is, I was able to respond to this one due to experience.

Unfortunately.

fox25news shared a link.

 Mass. urology practice offers pizza with vasectomy
www.myfoxboston.com

Get a vasectomy, eat some pizza and watch some basketball.

 Like · Comment · Share · 2 hours ago ·

 Rodney Lacroix Ironic that "thin sliced pepperoni" is the only option.
2 hours ago · Like · 👍 4

 Scott   All I got was blue balls, no pizza
2 hours ago · Unlike · 👍 1

 Rodney Lacroix After seeing smoke puffs rise from my crotch due
to cauterization, the last thing I was thinking about was a brick-oven
thin crust.
about an hour ago · Like · 👍 5

Honestly, I think a better option would have been for the urologist to offer a bag of frozen peas. Or Vicodin. Or a bag of frozen Vicodin.

Oh my God that sounds awesome.

applies for patent

Speaking of balls, a story appeared on my local Fox affiliate in which they said "riding a bike diminishes sexual pleasure for women." As luck would have it, it was my old friend Gene who broke the story.

Contrary to this story, I've stood outside a spin class and can tell you that watching a room full of woman riding bikes – their bums facing the viewing area – has the *opposite* effect on men. This also violates the gym's harassment policy and will get you thrown out.

Just in case you're having a tough time getting out of your gym contract, I offer that as a freebie. You're welcome.

Now ... about that biking story ...

> **mooooooog35** @mooooooog35   3h
> @fox25gene "Riding a bike diminishes sexual pleasure for women. Men everywhere go, "So?"" @shannonmulaire
> Expand

> **Gene Lavanchy** @fox25gene   2h
> @mooooooog35 @shannonmulaire It's why I sold my wife's bike!
> Hide conversation   Reply   Retweet   Favorite
>
> 6:30 AM - 15 May 12 via web · Details

> **mooooooog35** @mooooooog35   2h
> @fox25gene you'd think it would diminish pleasure for the man, too. Just trying to keep your balance would be a distraction @shannonmulaire
> Expand

So if you're a gym owner and suddenly women aren't signing up for your spin classes, now you probably know why. Sex just hasn't been the same. Either that, or they were tired of the little guy staring at their butts from the viewing area.

So now I'm stuck in this two-year gym contract with no discernible way out.

News stories suck sometimes.

That said, I highly recommend seeking out your favorite local news anchors and attempting to have your way with them.

I can tell you from experience that hot news anchors don't like direct Tweets or Facebook comments that say stuff like:

"Hey, I see you still have your pregnancy tits. O_O"

"I want to have sex with you so I can hear you say in your news anchor voice: *'This just in ...'*"

You will find yourself blocked, or in some cases, on the other side of a court summons and wearing ankle bracelets.

peers out window longingly hoping someday to breathe fresh air again

One last thing to avoid is saying creepy things like this to your local sexpot meteorologist:

WBZ | CBS Boston

Meteorologist Melissa Mack: Also, you can follow me on Twitter.

Melissa Mack (MackWBZ) on Twitter

👍 5 people like this.

Rodney Lacroix I already follow you. Just not on Twitter. *waves from bushes*
6 hours ago · Like · 👍 2 people

Chloe she probably audibly gasped while reading that last part of the comment. lol
19 minutes ago · Like

I don't know if she audibly gasped or not, Chloe.

I know she moved, though, and now does weather somewhere in Ohio.

Tread lightly, my friends, tread lightly. And see you on the news.

RELATIONSHIP STATUS: ANNOYED

"I am a hopeless romantic, and I love to spoil my girlfriends." - *Orlando Bloom*

"I have worshipped woman as the living embodiment of the spirit of service and sacrifice." - *Mahatma Gandhi*

"You know you're an asshole when your girlfriend says, 'I love you more' and you answer, 'Yeah, probably.'" - *me, yesterday*

A brief history ...

My fiancée and I met during my short, yet very successful (read: sex with strangers) stint on Match.com. Here's a brief story of how we met ...

I was into my 2nd or 3rd month on Match.com and going through the same old searches that everyone on there goes through. The thing about online dating is that when you first sign on, you're like, "Hey, I might as well ask for exactly what I want in a person," so everyone's initial criteria for what they are looking for in a mate looks something like this:

```
Woman looking for a Man: Very attractive, tall, sexy,
athletic, rugged, can build things, can kill spiders,
great sense of humor and can make me laugh. Must be
successful, enjoy romance, and love to travel.

Man looking for a Woman: Must have a vagina and
decent-sized boobs. No uni-brows, missing teeth, or
plate-sized nipples, please. Cooking a plus.
```

Then, after a while, when you finally realize that: (1) no one is answering your ad, or (2) the people who ARE answering your ad have nothing in common with what you've asked for, your criteria changes to something like this:

```
Woman looking for a Man: Must be bipedal and not
living with parents.
```

> Man looking for a woman: I don't care. Someone just
> suck this thing.

So I was at that point in my Match.com stint when I decided to expand my horizons and stop looking for the *perfect* match. Since you can say how tall you want your date to be, I figured that most women weren't finding me in their results because I'm roughly the height of an end table.

So I decided to look for a woman who was searching for a man outside my own height range of 5'-3" to 5'-5" (read: **no one**).

And that's when I saw THIS as one of the female profile pictures:

I laughed. Hard.

This? This TOOK BALLS, people.

I opened the profile and saw that this particular woman was looking for a man at least 5-9" tall. My heart dropped. But, I needed to let this woman know that she did, indeed, make me laugh. So I emailed her, even though I was below her height requirement by an inch or six, and told her she'd grabbed my attention. Then I asked her to grab **my** attention explaining that *"Attention"* was the name of my penis. Then I deleted that line in the email because a joke like that is best left for the initial phone call.

As I write this, we have been together for about three years and are engaged to be married less than a week after this book comes out.

crosses fingers

That said, you can only imagine the mountain of crap she's had to endure. Luckily, she has a great sense of humor – a requirement when you need to put up with someone like me on a daily (yet alone yearly) basis. The following examples of this – via our Instant Message conversations and Facebook updates – prove to underscore this point.

And if you're into giving sympathy checks, please make them payable to yours truly. I'll make sure she gets them.

Kerri and I talk to each other throughout the day using Instant Messages. I've gone through great lengths to make sure most of our conversation texts are encrypted because I'm pretty sure the use of the word **_"dildo"_** seventeen times in three minutes would throw up some red flags for my IT Department.

This particular conversation happened as I was contemplating getting a tattoo on one of my arms. I don't like pain or needles or painful needles, so this decision needed to be thought out with great care.

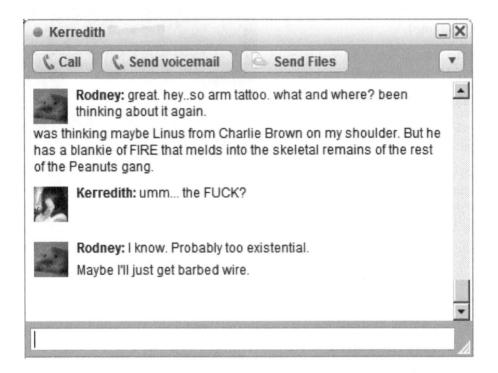

In the end, I didn't end up getting a tattoo because of the "pain" and "needles" thing. Plus, I couldn't find a tattoo studio that would put you under full anesthesia, and now that I'm writing that, I'm totally putting it in my *great-ideas-to-make-me-rich* book. It's the only thing in there right now, so it's more of a pamphlet, really.

The holidays rolled around soon after that, and I happened to be staying at Kerri's with my dog on Thanksgiving morning. Before I left to be with my kids for the day, I decided to spread the holiday joy, and of course, let all my friends on Facebook enjoy the festivities:

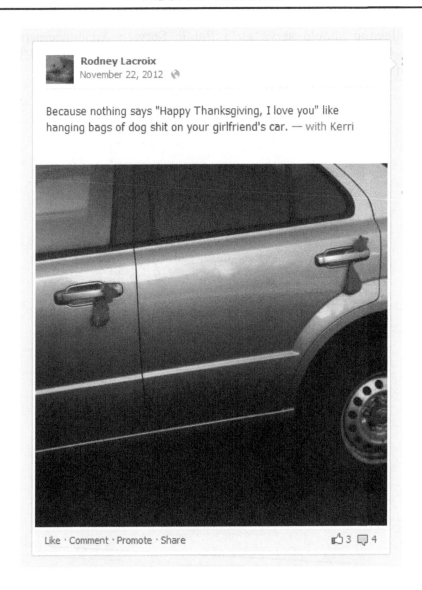

Rodney Lacroix
November 22, 2012

Because nothing says "Happy Thanksgiving, I love you" like hanging bags of dog shit on your girlfriend's car. — with Kerri

Like · Comment · Promote · Share   👍3 💬4

And then I drove away to go have turkey, leaving Kerri's car decorated with dangling bags of dog poop.

I think this falls under "love has no bounds" or "are you fucking kidding me?!"

Either is appropriate, really.

BRAIN NUGGET

WAS GOING TO GET ONE OF THOSE "LIVE, LAUGH, LOVE" WALL HANGINGS BUT MY HOUSE IS MORE OF A "YELL, FART, LAUGH" PLACE.

The following should serve as a Public Service Announcement to all girlfriends/fiancées/women: **DON'T TEXT YOUR MAN WHEN HE'S ON THE TOILET!**

Hey, she asked ...

My children are older now – as I sit here writing this, my daughter has just become a teenager and my son is now ten. This is a magical time because they are pretty self-sufficient and can be left to their own devices. Most of these devices are made by Apple. I wish they could buy their own devices because those things are expensive as hell.

In the case of my daughter, she has actually taken self-sufficiency one step further and grasped the initiative to yell at me whenever I ask her to do something. I'm pretty sure this is why I will not be opposed to "The Hunger Games" becoming a reality in the near future.

But Kerri's kids are pretty young and at ages where they don't have to try to be annoying. At age four, *being annoying* pretty much comes with the territory, and that can be directly attributed to parents wanting to teach their children how to walk and talk and interact.

Hindsight being 20/20, this is a stupid, stupid idea.

In a perfect world, children would learn to walk and talk at age eighteen, when you could then teach them how to walk to McDonald's and talk through a job interview so they could immediately move out of the house.

So when Kerri and I were in dating mode and living in separate houses, the simple task of me taking a shower at her place became an exercise in futility. A small child's bathroom is a like a mine field. Before you can even lather up, you must first maneuver yourself through the 354 toys scattered along the shower floor while trying NOT to knock down the squirt guns and giant bottles of watermelon shampoo lying on the shower shelves as you bend over.

Or, you could just leave them there and Tweet about the experience.

moooooog35 @moooooog35
I like when my girlfriend's kids leave their toys in the bathtub. It's always nice to have targets to pee on when I'm taking a shower.

Kerredith
@moooooog35 peeing on Ariel is a little creepy babe.

moooooog35 @moooooog35
@Kerredith615 says you. she looked like she quite enjoyed it.

I never really had a thing for gingers, but once you pee on one you're kind of hooked.

Ah, romance.

Men, if you're looking for advice on how to spontaneously woo your woman through creative instant messaging ...

...this probably isn't it:

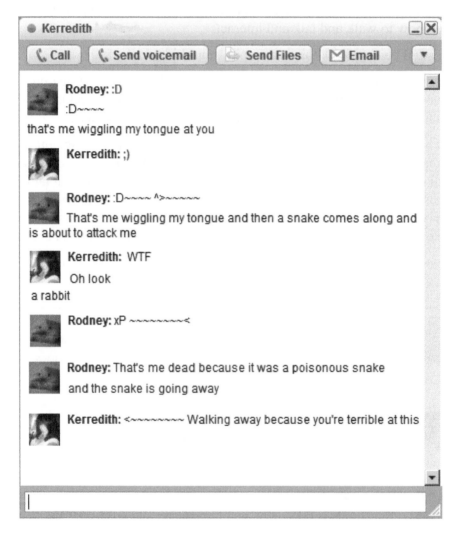

One of the best things about having a life partner is having someone who stands beside you, through thick or thin, and has your back no matter what.

So I've heard.

On one particular morning, I walked directly into a spider web while I was getting onto my motorcycle in the garage. I freaked out for thirty minutes making sure there wasn't a spider on me ... by completely undressing and taking a shower and then setting my clothes on fire, and of course, writing about it on Facebook.

Then I rode to work and it somehow GOT WORSE.

 Rodney: worst. spider morning. in history.

Sent at 8:54 AM on Friday

 Kerredith: I saw that.. HAHAHAHAHA

wuss

 Rodney: NO

THERE IS MORE

I drop Cam off at school on the motorcycle and start heading to work

as I'm at a stop light at the mall, I look down and ANOTHER ONE OF THESE SPIDERS crawls out from my front fork nut.

Like..just in front of my gas tank.

It had a BLUE BUM.

I'm like, 'Please no wind please no wind please no wind' and he crawled back into the little cubby he was hiding but every time I stopped he'd peek back out just to fuck with me.

Got to work and then coaxed him out with a stick and then stomped that fucker like I was an Irish step dancer.

 Kerredith:
hahahahahahahahahahahahahahahahahahahah
hahahahahahaha

Sent at 9:01 AM on Friday

 Kerredith: I mean.

OMG.. that's terrible

you poor thing

Ugh

LOL

 Rodney: hate you sometimes.

So, yeah. Now accepting applications for one of those life partners who stands behind you no matter what. Especially if they'll kill spiders for me. Email for details. Include boob pics.

Then there are the IMs that have no rhyme or reason other than I feel like giving Kerri a WTF moment for her day.

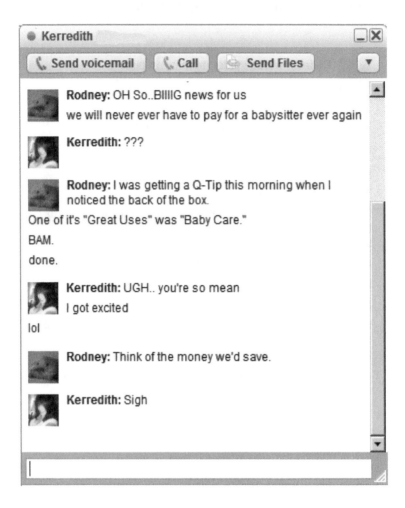

Turns out that Q-Tips kind of drop the ball when the kids are choking on food. You'd think they'd have that warning on the package. Weird.

THE FAMILY THAT PRANKS TOGETHER ...

The original title of this section was "Screwing with Kids," but my publisher felt this would probably draw the wrong crowd. I kind of agreed with him but put forth the argument that "sales are sales" which was followed him saying, "Dude. What is WRONG with you?" so then it was tentatively titled "The Only Argument for Having Children," which I thought satisfied both parties. You can see it's been changed again because editors are assholes.

As you are well aware, one of my greatest joys of being a father is being able to lie to my children. As my kids have gotten older, this has changed into having actual conversations which – in all honesty – kind of sucks.

If I wanted to have an adult conversation with someone, I'd call a 900 number.

However, the best part of my kids being older is that they have learned the art of being smart-asses themselves. And I end up writing most of our conversations down, so I can share them with others. Also, I'm old and forget things pretty quickly. Also, I'm old and forget things pretty quickly.

Case in point:

Rodney Lacroix
September 24, 2012 at 6:32pm ·

Conversation with my boy:

Me: "Hey. Do you think I'm a good daddy?"
Cam: "You're the best. Who wouldn't want a dad like you?"
Me: "Thanks buddy. You know I'm not paying you for saying that, right?"
Cam: "Awww crap."

My son has somehow managed to become the patriarch comic of the family. He draws better than I do, has better comedic timing than I do, and is a threat to my leadership. I predict there will come a time when we will have a competition in biting a woman's face to see which of us the female deems the Alpha. That's probably not right. There's a Discovery Channel special on sea otters right now playing in the background so I might be confusing how this works. I guess we'll find out when we start biting faces. THEN IT'S ON.

So I take whatever opportunities I can to give my son some old-fashioned ribbing. An example of this is in the following conversation about my dog. Jax is not a kissy-feely kind of dog. He's more of a "pat me and maybe I'll look in your general vicinity" kind of dog. So he's more like a cat but without the "I'm an asshole" personality.

So, when Jax does give kisses, it's kind of a big deal around here.

Rodney Lacroix
September 14, 2012 at 6:49am ·

Jax was lying on the chair licking Cam's hand.

Cam: "Look daddy! Jax is giving me kisses!"
Me: "..Or do you think he's seeing what you taste like so he can eat you in your sleep?"
Cam: "Stop it!" *pulls hand away

Yeah. I'm still Alpha. For now.

bites Kerri's face just to make sure

Alpha male status gives me the freedom to try out new material on my children. The best time for doing this is in the car because the comedy distracts my kids from trying to grab the wheel while I'm simultaneously writing these jokes in my notepad and driving 45 mph with my knees. It's like my children only care about their safety and nothing about my writing career. Yeah. Keep grabbing that wheel. Hope you enjoy not going to college, guys.

My kids and I were driving past my church one day when we noticed the sign out front:

"Comic Night"

Keep in mind that driving by my church is about as close as my family gets to going into one, so the fact that the church was having a night with comics kind of got our attention. I immediately thought up a Tweet and posted:

BRAIN NUGGET

KIDS AND I SPENT OUR ENTIRE DINNER AT THE RESTAURANT SWITCHING SEATS EVERY TIME THE WAITRESS LEFT. VERY ENTERTAINING. HIGHLY RECOMMENDED.

"My church is having a comedy night. I'm sure if I went, my jokes would bring the house down. WITH LIGHTNING."

cricket

The following conversation with my kids ensued seconds later in the car:

Rodney Lacroix
Saturday at 4:43pm via mobile ·

Conversation with my kids in the car about the church's "Comic Night."

Me: "I Tweeted that if I went, my jokes would bring the house down. WITH LIGHTNING."

*cricket

Daughter: "I don't get it."

Son: "Me either."

Me: "God would strike with lightning. Cuz he'd be mad."

Son: "OH. Like the time he had a fit when Jesus died."

Me: "What?!"

Son: "Yeah. He had a fit that Jesus died. That's what caused the earthquake."

Me: "What earthquake!?"

Son: "Of 1997."

Me: "We are all going to Hell."

Yep. All going to hell. And if they keep grabbing at my steering wheel, they're going to have to pay their own way, too. Hopefully, meals are included.

Meals. As an intro to this next one, I have to tell you that my kids normally don't try anything new. The majority of their diet consists of chicken nuggets and chicken nugget-shaped by-products that may or may not contain chicken or nuggets or any non-human protein, in general.

And milk.

I believe in good nutrition.

I'm always trying to get my kids to expand their taste buds. This inevitably fails, unless of course it's a new strain of chicken nugget.

The following conversation happened one night while I was coaxing my kids to try something I was eating (which they declined):

Rodney Lacroix
January 24

Supper conversations:

Cam: "I remember one time you grounded me for not trying ham."
Me: "Um. That doesn't sound like me."
*Cam nods
Me: "I don't think I'd ground you just because you didn't like ham."
Cam: "Yes. I told you that I didn't like pink foods and you grounded me."
Me: *dying
Payton: "I don't think I've ever been grounded."
Cam: "I've been grounded plenty of times for not trying pink food."

On the rare occasion that my kids are not eating chicken nuggets, I get them to eat steak. On this particular evening, I told them we were having rib eye steaks.

... and thus it unfolded ...

Rodney Lacroix
July 26, 2012 at 8:02pm near Salem · 🌐

Talking about steak tonight with the kids.

Payton: "Wait. What's rabbi steak, again?"
Me: "It's rib eye. Not rabbi."
Payton: "Oh yeah. A rabbi is a disease that makes dogs crazy."
Me: "No. That's rabies."
Cam: "Payton, a rabbi is a Chinese judge."
Me: "Um. No. Close, though. A rabbi is a Jewish priest."
Cam: "I knew it was something like that."

OMG I love my kids.

Speaking of going to hell, I'm kind of hoping that decision is not made by rabbis, rib eyes, or even Chinese judges because at least one of those saw the above conversation. This is assuming that the rabbi has Internet and can read my Facebook page.

I think I'm safe on the Chinese judge because everyone knows that Chinese people are restricted to only two web sites in their country and both of them are related to Pokemon or Hello Kitty.

I'm starting to think I should probably pay more attention to the actual stories on the news instead of just making wiseass comments to the anchors and looking at the female meteorologist's boobs.

Nah.

There's a reason I got this laptop, and damn if I'm not going to use it the way I please. Sadly, the way I please is for porn and porn-related searches. And because of that, I've had to retype this entire book three times due to viruses and boob pop-ups.

Boob pop-ups: yay.

Viruses: notsomuch.

That brings us to technology. My kids were born in an age of cable television, iPods, iPhones, and iCarly.

And of course, I was not. I was born in the age of antenna television and *I-Can't-Get-This-Station-To-Come-In-Even-Using-Aluminum-Foil-Rabbit-Ears*. This can be hard for children to comprehend.

Case in point:

Rodney Lacroix
November 1, 2012

Watching "Poltergeist" with the kids the other night when they start with the scene where the TV goes to static.

Me (pausing the TV to explain): "That's what happened every night when the TV stations shut down."
Daughter: "Why?"
Me: "They didn't have 24-hour programming. Everyone at the station would go home and the TV would come back on in the morning sometime."
Son: "Were you alive back then?"
Me: "Sadly, yes."
Daughter: "Oh my God you are SO old."

Yeah. Tell me about it.

Like · Comment · Promote · Share   👍 30 💬 12

Nothing says "I love you dad" like kids hammering you about your age. My favorite is when I'm sitting on the floor and my daughter is on the couch poking my head:

"Bald spot. Bald spot. Bald spot. Bald spot."

My kids love me.

BRAIN NUGGET

I'M NOT HOMOPHOBIC
UNLESS YOU COUNT
GAY SPIDERS.

Sorry. My kids love MAKING FUN OF me. There. That's more accurate.

On the bright side, the older I get, the closer I am to being incontinent and making them have to change my poopy diapers. So there's a silver lining to parenting after all.

With my luck, that silver lining is lined with spiders. Ah, spiders.

Not only does the entire free world know that I have arachnophobia, but my children have a keen sense of this also. Couple that with a twelve-year-old smartass holding an iPhone, and I get crap like this:

Rodney Lacroix · 91 followers
21 hours ago near Salem ·

My daughter just texted me a picture of a spider. A "SMILING Spider." (trust me, it's not effing smiling).

I text back: "GAH!"

She texts back: "Dad!! I was in the middle of a music video!! Text me back in 10 minutes. Please. Don't reply back to this yet. Reply back in 10 minutes."

So, she texts ME a picture of a spider and I'm the bad guy for texting her back an interrupting her music video?!?

At least, that's what I asked when I texted her back immediately.

:)

She immediately called to yell at me for texting her.

I was not surprised at this because my daughter has my temperament. By "she has my temperament" I mean "she can be really mean and yells a lot."

From the time she started talking, my daughter has only had six hours of *not speaking*. And most of that time was when she was drinking something because we've learned she can't talk and drink at the same time

But the skill of talking while eating is one she has mastered.

I've seen so much chewed-up food from talking with my kids that I could probably give lectures at Harvard on the scientific principles of pre-digestion.

One day my kids were sitting around watching television when an ad for "Stuffies" came on. Stuffies are those giant stuffed animal pillow things that unzip, allowing your kids to shove all kinds of crap inside them.

Rodney Lacroix
December 1, 2012 near Salem

Watching a commercial for "Stuffies" stuffed animals with all kinds of hidden, closeable pockets.

Me: "I wish you guys had one of those."
Son: "A Stuffie?"
Me: "No. A mouth with a zipper on it."

Like · Comment · Promote · Share   👍 19 💬 1

If I invented this, parents would buy these things by the DOZENS.

light bulb

(Writes down in "get rich" book ...)

Yet, even with zippered mouths, my kids never have a hard time expressing themselves. Shortly after my first book came out, I got a new tattoo.

I've been talking about that tattoo, and I know you're curious. It's a fire-breathing dragon that works my kids' initials (C & P) into the design. If you have two kids, you know that the two-headed dragon part is self-explanatory.

Anyway, the tattoo was on my upper back, so I needed someone else to lotion it till it healed (the curse that comes with having massive, kissable biceps). Since none of the Dallas Cowboy Cheerleaders were available to apply my lotion, I asked my daughter who – obviously – had no issues with it:

Rodney Lacroix
December 20, 2012 at 9:44pm near Salem ·

I just asked my daughter to put lotion on my touched-up tattoo.

Her: "I can't believe you have to do this."
Me: "I know."
Her: "No. I mean I can't believe *I* have to do this."

Then there is my son. Sometimes he can be pure genius.

Whenever I do a radio interview, I always make sure people know that the real comedians in my house are my children. How they come up with some of the stuff they do amazes me.

Perfect example:

Rodney Lacroix · 91 followers
11 hours ago near Salem ·

Was at an appointment with my daughter. My son came along.

At one point, my daughter and I were called into the office while my son waited outside with his notebook and pencil.

We were in the office for a VERY long time.

We opened the door and there was Cam, pretending to sleep in the chair, arms crossed...

....and a paper beard fastened to his chin.

I can tell you that if you've never exited an appointment to find your son sitting in a chair with a homemade paper beard attached to his chin – as if he'd been there for twenty years – then you haven't lived.

It's moments like those I wish my mind had a video camera attached to it so I could record my life for posterity. I would call it "Go-Ogle Glasses." You could wear them and do all kinds of cool Internet stuff like watch porn (hence the "Go-Ogle") while jaywalking into fountains.

I hope no one steals that idea.

(scribbles into "get rich book")

BRAIN NUGGET

THEY SAY "A BUTTERFLY FLAPPING
ITS WINGS IN CHINA CAN CAUSE A
TORNADO IN THE GREAT PLAINS."
HELP SAVE LIVES.
KILL A BUTTERFLY TODAY.

Rodney Lacroix
December 2, 2012 near Salem

Instant message from my daughter tonight:

Her: "Daddy. Daddy, you there?"
Me: "Hey honey. What's up?"
Her: "Nothing. I was bored and looking for something to do, and Kate and Becca weren't around."
Me: "Always nice to know I'm your 3rd choice."
Her: "Hey. At least you're in the top 3."

That's my girl.

Like · Comment · Promote · Share   👍 31 💬 2

... and that's how she fell out of my Top Two.

Rodney Lacroix
After walking through Boston today, my daughter looked tired.

Me: "You tired?"

Payt: "Yeah. It's from all the walking in the cold."

Me: "You know, you burn more calories walking in cold than you do walking in warm weather."

Payt: "Really?"

Me: "Yep. Do you know why?"

Payt: "Because you end up running to get somewhere to get out of the cold."

I can't argue with that logic.

MESSING WITH CO-WORKERS
OR
I PUT THE "COW" IN COWORKER

Some facts for you:

- *The average person spends 90,000 hours at work over their lifetime.*

- *80% of people are dissatisfied with their jobs.*

- *People spend 2,760 hours laughing during our lives.*

- *99% of people still don't understand why Prince changed his name to that squiggly symbol thing.*

My goal when I get to work each morning is to do just enough to not get fired. In order to do this, I have to do something that resembles real work during the course of a day.

However, because I have a pretty short attention span and don't like to work, this presents a problem. In fact, my publisher told me to add a bunch of intros into this section and it's taken me two days so far and all of it is crap.

This is mainly because I've been wandering around, texting, eating pita chips, playing Candy Crush, and losing my mind every time I look out the window because I forget a spider plant is hanging there and it freaks me the hell out.

Arachnophobia knows no bounds.

Luckily for me, I've had the pleasure of dealing with pretty decent people at my jobs. Most – if not all – can take a joke. This is a necessity because I have a ***need*** to make my job fun, usually at the expense of others. Again, you shouldn't be surprised at all if you've read this far.

One of my female coworkers was getting married last year.

Side Note: When you work in the computer industry, "female" and "coworker" don't usually go together, so I felt the need to write "female coworker" here. Working in the tech industry is akin to working at a steel mill where you're generally surrounded by all men. The exception to this is the token hot chick who wears cutoff jean shorts, ties her shirt in a knot, pours water on her face, then looks over at you – sultry and pouty – and licks her lips really, really slowly.

You've just been given a glimpse of my happy place.

Well. One of them.

Regardless: Female coworker + Bachelorette party = ...

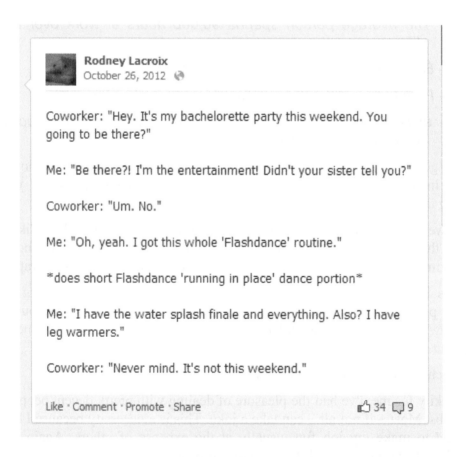

Rodney Lacroix
October 26, 2012

Coworker: "Hey. It's my bachelorette party this weekend. You going to be there?"

Me: "Be there?! I'm the entertainment! Didn't your sister tell you?"

Coworker: "Um. No."

Me: "Oh, yeah. I got this whole 'Flashdance' routine."

does short Flashdance 'running in place' dance portion

Me: "I have the water splash finale and everything. Also? I have leg warmers."

Coworker: "Never mind. It's not this weekend."

Like · Comment · Promote · Share   👍 34 💬 9

But first, let's back up a bit. It should be duly noted here that she is Egyptian, even though she worked in a cubical and not high atop the crest of a Sphinx as one would expect. Weird. I don't understand some cultures.

(Also please note my sweet Google email profile photo that week: the dude from Flock of Seagulls)

It appears that my editor has no problem changing my damn titles around but can't put stories in correct order. I would bitch, but then I'd have to do all the work myself. Speaking up seems stupid at this point.

So my female coworker with the bachelorette party? Her name is Engy, obviously.

BRAIN NUGGET

MY ONLINE BANKING HOMEPAGE HAS A WOMAN SMILING. HONEY, I'M SEEING HOW BADLY I'M OVERDRAWN. WIPE THAT GODDAMN SMIRK OFF YOUR FACE.

She did not invite me to her wedding, which is fine because I don't usually like churches and/or weddings.

Also, Engy was really religious which means that her wedding would have been more torture than the usual wedding. Religion = torture. I know this because I read about the Crusades once. Or maybe it was a Monty Python movie. Honestly, I can't remember, but as a devout Catholic, I have been to church a handful of times and it really sucks.

"Devout" here actually means "awful."

Still, when Engy took some time off for her upcoming nuptials, I posted this to her Facebook wall.

 Rodney Lacroix ▶ Engy

Good luck this weekend!! OH - I've been going around the office asking everyone if they were going to your wedding and if they said 'no' I said "Wow. I think you're the only one in the building not going." Long story short, you may have to repair some friendships when you come back to work. Have fun!!!

I'm such a good coworker.

I'm also very lucky to have a boss with a great sense of humor. So great, in fact, that he bought my first book. Granted, it didn't have nearly the amount of content about me screwing off at work as this one does.

I should probably fire up my resume skills in the event he buys this one too.

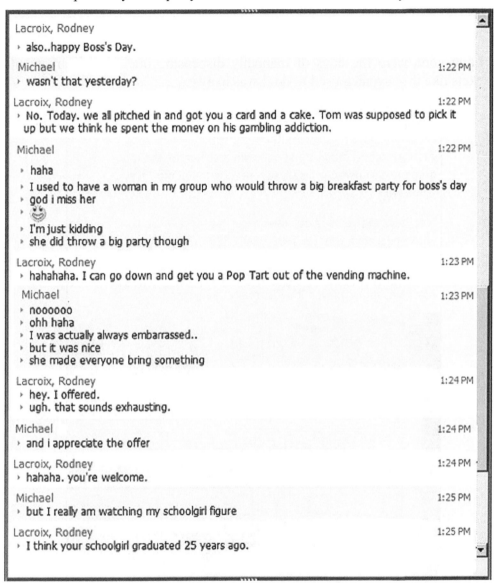

When my work moved into a new building, one of the first things we got was a new cafeteria and coffee area.

I take my coffee very seriously because if I don't have coffee in the morning, there is a distinct chance I will begin killing random people for no reason. This is a chance everyone normally takes with me anyway, but without coffee in the morning, the percentage increases exponentially.

So my joy was overwhelming when I realized that our little sugar packets were replaced with an automatic sugar dispenser.

AN AUTOMATIC SUGAR DISPENSER.

Long gone were the days of manually dispensing our own sugar out of packets like the cavemen used to do. I was in awe.

And now that I look at the picture, I think I'm more worried about the difference between "Sugar" and "All Natural Sugar." Sometimes I'll make a huge coffee with a little "Splenda," "Blue Sweetener," and regular "Sugar" just to thumb my nose at the "All Natural Sugar" sitting all there all high and mighty with its reusable grocery bags and recycling bins and Prius.

No one likes a hippie sweetener, Natural Sugar.

And finally, all of you who "work from home" will get this next montage without any more explaining needed:

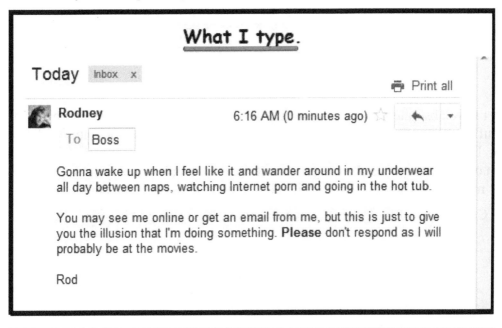

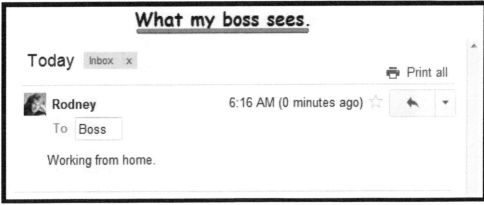

A CORNUCOPIA OF FUDGERY

I have absolutely no idea what this title means except that here's a bunch of stuff I can't categorize anywhere else: replies to news posts or status updates or Tweets that just write themselves in my head. You may even find yourself on one of these pages, or recognize a story, or get a paper cut turning the page or maybe get a smudge on your Kindle. Seriously, dude. Get a napkin.

Cornucopia of Fudgery: You never know what's going to happen.

 WCVB Channel 5 Boston
Yesterday

Hey EyeOpener friends. Here's the one that has us talking this morning: Burger King is launching a "bacon sundae" nationwide. 510 calories...19 grams of fat. Does this take fast food too far?

Rodney Lacroix Instead of crowns, Burger King is now passing out inflated angioplasty balloons.
Yesterday at 6:05am · Like · 👍 4

Meleah

Um ... What's the first thing that comes to your mind when you see the words "bone marrow abnormality?"

Rodney Lacroix That you said 'bone.'
39 minutes ago · Like · 👍 7

(it's all about the sex, people)

Z104 WNVZ
Anybody wanna finish the joke for us??
Like · Comment · Share · 4 hours ago

Anita we cantelope
4 hours ago · Like

Adrianna I cantaloupe.
4 hours ago · Like

Rodney Lacroix "You're seedless and I've always wanted a family."
3 hours ago · Like · 👍 6

Brad   14m
@ChelseaKrost Expose yourself to your deepest fear, after that fear
has no power.

moooooog35 @moooooog35   12m
@lefty9876 @chelseakrost I fear spiders. With all due respect, screw
that.

Chelsea Krost @ChelseaKrost   12m
@moooooog35 @lefty9876 I don't like spiders either lol.

moooooog35 @moooooog35   2m
@ChelseaKrost Liking spiders is unnatural. Like not liking bacon. Or
being vegan. Or being vegan and not liking bacon. That seems
redundant.

On a related note, Chelsea Krost is pretty hot so I've been trying to become her biggest fear so she exposes herself to me.

So far, no luck.

Keep your fingers crossed.

Amy
20 minutes ago near Salem ·

Holy shit! Ground cloves are expensive!!

Rodney Lacroix That's why I buy air cloves.
15 minutes ago · Like · 👍 1

hook reaches in and yanks me off stage

Rodney Lacroix
November 20, 2012 at 9:44am · ⊕

Text conversation with my buddy, Bobby Goldman, this morning about my upcoming book:

Me: "Call me. I have BIG NEWS."
Rob: "Are you getting married?"
Me: "No. Call me."
Rob: "You pregnant?"
Me: "NO. Dude. CALL ME."
Rob: "Going to Hedonism?"
Me: "No. I wish. Great. Now I'm depressed."

Seriously, Bobby. Way to deflate my goddamn balloon.

Anne
A lovely added bonus...

Like · Comment · Share · 13 minutes ago · 🙎

 Rodney Lacroix I have that same sign over my bed!
10 minutes ago · Like

Rodney Lacroix
August 30, 2012

My birthday present from my beautiful girlfriend, Kerri, and the typical conversation we have that followed.

Me: "Awesome. But why is this 'Life is Crap?'"
Kerri: "Um. The girl is falling off the motorcycle?"
Me: "Again. Why is this a crappy thing?"
Kerri (sigh): "Oh, look. The driver is BALD."
Me: "Oh, look. The girl HAS BOOBS."
Kerri: "..."
Me: "Maybe THAT'S why life is crap. Because my girlfriend-slash-mistress with boobs fell off my bike."
Kerri: "grrr"
Me (whispering): "You can't win."

And now for a post that had to be majorly condensed ... a woman who did not like (or read) my first book ... but felt the need to personally bash me.

Rodney Lacroix

"Hysterical!" - Jenny McCarthy

My adult humor book, "Things Go Wrong for Me," has a bunch of stories from my childhood that happened RIGHT ON ABBOTT STREET in Lawrence!!

With over 90% of my 126 Amazon reviews being 4 or 5-star, 6 consecutive weeks on Amazon's Best Seller list and in stunning full color in both paperback and Kindle versions, I hope you'll give it a read!

http://bit.ly/12o6h8N

Things Go Wrong For Me (when life hands you lemons, add vodka)
www.amazon.com

Things Go Wrong For Me is a memoir of sorts, a road map of Rodney Lacroix's haywire life thus far. From his childhood, through the raising of his own kids, to his vasectomy and post-divorce world ... this book is more than just a culmination of outrageous stories woven

Like · Comment · Unfollow Post · Share · Saturday at 2:58pm near Salem

Linda   Horrible book.
5 hours ago · Like

Brian   wow..smackdown..I like the title...
5 hours ago · Like

Linda   way to tear on your kids....
4 hours ago · Like

Rodney Lacroix Thank you, Linda. You sound nice.
4 hours ago · Like

Linda   As nice as a guy who uses his real kids names as he tears them down and a shot of the house his kids live in in a book he publishes for anyone to pick up.
3 hours ago · Like

Rodney Lacroix You seem angry. Have we had sex before? Because that would totally explain everything. That being said, feel free to add your review on Amazon as a 1-star. All reviews are welcome. You can put it there with the other 3. Just below the 102 5-star and 13- 4 star ones. Thank you in advance!
3 hours ago · Like

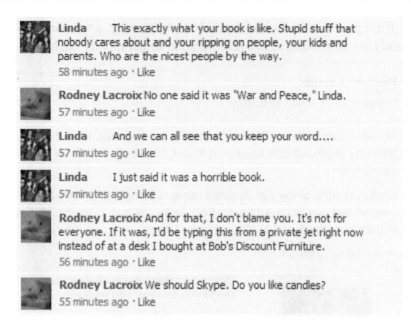

Linda This exactly what your book is like. Stupid stuff that nobody cares about and your ripping on people, your kids and parents. Who are the nicest people by the way.
58 minutes ago · Like

Rodney Lacroix No one said it was "War and Peace," Linda.
57 minutes ago · Like

Linda And we can all see that you keep your word....
57 minutes ago · Like

Linda I just said it was a horrible book.
57 minutes ago · Like

Rodney Lacroix And for that, I don't blame you. It's not for everyone. If it was, I'd be typing this from a private jet right now instead of at a desk I bought at Bob's Discount Furniture.
56 minutes ago · Like

Rodney Lacroix We should Skype. Do you like candles?
55 minutes ago · Like

This is also why it's fruitless to argue with me, because I always turn angry attacks against me into an attempt to get a Swedish massage.

Kristin
5 minutes ago via mobile ·

Just had a very very big kitty in the backyard

Rodney Lacroix Weird. The men's room wall says you have a very very big kitty, too.
2 minutes ago · Like

That's Kristin, a former co-worker. In my defense, it did say that on the men's room wall but only because I wrote it there.

K-Rock's Rock Alarm @rockalarm 22m
Monday's T.i.T. question: About 80% of us have never been here in a decade. Where? #RockAlarm #Trivia

mooooooog35 @mooooooog35 16m
@rockalarm Funkytown?

S.P.A.M E.M.A.I.L.
(Some People Are Mean.
Even Manly Assholes.
Introducing, Lacroix.)

Sometimes? Sometimes you just have to.

Oh. You're a millionaire in Haiti? But you're sick and can't get your money out? You need my help? I just have to wire a few thousand for processing fees? What am I wearing? You tell me first. What are you wearing? Shaved. You? Oh, you like to be spanked with sock monkeys? Me too. Once, I had a llama and ...

GAH.

Sorry. This is what happens when I have a chat window open at the same time I'm writing chapter introductions.

Where was I? Oh.

Sometimes? Sometimes you just have to ... you just have to **REPLY**.

We've all gotten the emails. Sad stories. Heartfelt tales. All in terrible, terrible English – this is because all the emails are generated by trained ocelots in Jamaica which is, as we know, owned by the French, and those kind of literate ocelots have no respect for America.

And no matter how many times you mark email as "spam" or put addresses on "block lists" or "unsubscribe" to "people eating licorice socks" websites, the emails keep on coming. And coming. And coming. Like Mark Wahlberg in "Boogie Nights" but with more email and less prosthetic giant wangle donger.

Then you find that your grandmother's bank accounts are drained and now she's homeless because she made the mistake of leaving her bank card on her counter and there was **no way** you were risking your own account. Not again.

Eventually, you can't take it anymore. Despite everything the news has told you about replying to these emails, you think about doing it any way. Let's give those French-typing ocelots a taste of their own medicine!

Let's take Jamaica back and give it to the people of, I guess, Jamaica? New Zealand? It's in the Pacific, right? Is it a state or a country?

Jesus Christ, I suck at geography. Wait. My son just told me he thinks an ocelot is a fish. This has just gotten really creepy if he's right.

Doesn't matter. We reach our spam tolerance limits and reply with all the fervor and fortitude of Sir William Wallace getting his weenie tugged off at the end right after he yells "FREEDOM!" but just before they lop his head off, because, OW DUDE.

We release ourselves from the email tyranny and fight back with our own ocelots!! We fight back with our very own spam!

Well ... at least, I do.

My grandmothers are dead, and their accounts are long gone. Good luck with those, suckers.

Enjoy.

BRAIN NUGGET

SITTING IN A RESTAURANT
MAKING FUN OF A GUY
WEARING SUNGLASSES.
THEN HE GRABBED HIS
WIFE'S ARM, HIS CANE, AND LEFT.
WOOPS.

MS SHARON WILFRED WANTS MY LOVE SHAFD

The affair started oh-so innocently from just a simple email in my inbox:

Please note that the fact this came from the email address of "LoveShafd" did not escape me.

Things like this tend to catch my eye, so I sat and said "loveshafd" out loud for five minutes and giggled and sang it to the tune of "Love Shack" because I'm twelve and bore easily.

I was at work when I received this email, and I really didn't feel like working, so how could I ignore Ms. Sharon Wilfred?

What's the worst thing that could happen, I'd get my bank account wiped out? The reward of gaining a new friend was worth the risk losing that twenty bucks.

So I replied.

Hi Ms Sharon Wilfred!

Or ... can I just call you Sharon? Are we at that point in this relationship yet?

Sharon? Shar? Sharry?

OMG I love the song "Oh Sherrie" by Steve Perry (the guy from Journey with the great voice but unfortunately large nose). But you know what they say about guys with long noses, right?

If you do, please let me know ... because I kind of made that up but now I'm curious if there really is a saying.

So ... you want to be friends? Like pen pals? Or like a pet rock?

FYI - speaking of pet rocks, I have one googly eye. Always keep 'em guessing, that's what I always say. Am I looking at you? At a star? Passing vehicle? YOU NEVER KNOW WITH ME AND MY GOOGLY EYE!!

I be crazy.

I hope you like crazy. Cuz you just bought yourself a great big bucket of it, Shar. I'm crazy. I'm crazy for YOU. I know we've only known each other for, like, 5 paragraphs but I feel a connection to you that I haven't felt for a woman named Sharon Wilfred in a very long time.

I hope you feel the same.

I just touched my crotch.

I'm looking forward to our friendship gifts. What are they? Are they rings? Juggling balls? HAHAHA. I said 'balls.' Does that turn you on? It turns me on. Not the balls thing, the juggling thing. Jugglers are hot.

Trust me. I know. I'm one of them.

I just winked at you but you wouldn't know it, because of my googly eye.

Can't wait to have a sleepover. We can make popcorn and wear feety jammies. I'm so excited Shar. I'm so excited my nose just got HUGE.

Steve Perry gets that joke.

I WILL LOVE YOU FOREVER.

With love on this Kwanzaa,

Rodney

Then I sent it.

And then I did what I normally do at work, which is go the bathroom sixteen times and randomly walk by my boss' desk in a hurried fashion while mumbling some technological jargon like, "I can't believe the IP stack is crashing the java code with an exception and firewall popup blocker anti-virus laptop," which makes it appear like I know what I'm doing.

These helpful work tips are complimentary with your purchase of this book.

TOP 10 WAYS TO LOOK BUSY AT WORK:

1. *Walk really fast when you're going anywhere as to appear something important is going to happen.*
2. *Carry a notebook with you at all times. Seems like you are supposed to be somewhere taking notes. If at your desk, keep it open with a pen on it.*
3. *Keep your headset on if you are in your cubicle.*
4. *Actually do work, but that defeats the purpose. Right?*
5. *Shuffle Papers. (thanks shivani)*
6. *Look pissed off. (thanks shivani)*
7. *Put up a Do Not Disturb sign when you are browsing the web.*
8. *Continually click on a pen.*
9. *Walk around with your laptop open. Bonus: Take your laptop home and say you are Working From Home.*
10. *Open up Microsoft Word and write blog entries to post later. **

* MOST IMPORTANT ONE.

I totally wasn't expecting a reply from Ms Sharon Wilfred except ...

INBOX (1)

She replied.

HOLY CRAP SHE REPLIED.

Hi,

Dear i want you to know that, Distance, country, or any biological nature, age is number what matters most is love and affection. I will need a serious relationship that will last.

I am constrained to contact you, because of the maltreatment I, am receiving from my step mother. She planned to take away all my late father's treasury and properties from me since the unexpected death of my beloved Father.

My father secretly deposited the sum of US$7,823,000.00 in Senegal.

It is my intention to compensate you with 30% of the total money for your services and the balance shall be my investment capital.

Please below are the information's i needed from you to put things into action.

1. Your Full Name ....
2. You're Age ....
3. Your Occupation................
4. Your Home And Office Address...........
5. Your Telephone And Fax Number...........
6. Your picture...........

I am waiting for your confirmation of this mail to enable us discuss details, agreed and give you bank contact where the money was deposited.

Thanks as I hope to receive from you soon.

Yours Sincerely,

Miss. Sharon Wilfred.

DAMMIT, IT'S A SCAM.

My luck sucks.

No romance. No friendship. Just more nights of me sitting home watching Food Network crying sheepishly into a big bowl of hummus.

NEVAR ROME ALONE

I have no idea why I put this picture here.

So I wrote her back again:

Hi Shar!

This sounds like an excellent plan!!

I will do all of this if you kindly tell me whether or not you bang on the first date and, if so, if you'll let me go all raw dog on you. That would be nice, since my sores are almost all in remission!

Sucks about your step mom. Let me tell you, I've been there, done that. Not getting beaten, but more of a pay-for-submissiveness thing and it required me converting money to Canadian.

ANNOYING.

Is she, like, beating you? Do you have any video of this? If not, can you describe it in graphic detail, because I will make flip-book sketches that I can use to masturbate to later and we can use the money from your dead father (may he rest in peace) to start a porn business.

BIG. BUCKS. IN AMERICAN PORN.

Trust me. I'm a former child actor.

Love you, you crazy rich stepchild you.

Let me know about the banging thing. It's an important step in keeping this relationship rolling.

Forever your girl,

Rodney

It was only after I sent it that I realized item #6 on her list of things she wanted from me was a picture.

She requested my picture.

So I looked back at her email and lo and behold ...

... she had previously attached a picture of HERSELF:

Ladies and gentlemen, the lovely Ms. Sharon Wilfred!

Honestly, she looks pretty good for a victim of stepmom abuse.

And I, not one to disappoint the lovely Miss Sharon Wilfred, decided to send her an email with the pictures of me she originally requested:

```
OMG OMG SHARON!!

I forgot. You wanted a picture of me!

I only have a picture of me with my friend, Juan, who
I met at Hedonism when I was tricked to go there by
that Canadian person who took my wallet but that's a
different story for a different time and you and I have
forever together to discuss such trivial things.

You complete me.

So. I'm attaching a picture of me and Juan. Here you
go:
```

And so you have a better picture of our happy future together, you hot piece of ass you, I took the liberty of including a picture of the two of us looking blissfully happy and probably with a brood of several children and maybe a ferret.

```
OMG I LOVE ferrets.
They tickle going in. You'll see.
Muchos deneiros, my love!
Rodney
```

I received a single reply back a few days later from my beloved Ms. Sharon Wilfred. It simply said:

Your friend.

Friend? After all we'd been through, all the hopes and dreams we'd shared, my love was simply boiled down to a two-word reply: "Your friend." ??

I wrote her back:

```
    Friends don't stick swords in other people's bums,
Sharon. Lovers do. Lovers stick things in their other
lover's bum. I read that on a Valentine Candy Heart
once. I wrote it there. I had to write really tiny
using the sharpened end of a spoon because they don't
give you pens in prison. Also, Randall says 'hi.'
```

After that, the emails stopped coming.

I hope she's just being beaten by her stepmom like a little foreign Cinderella and not heartbroken or anything. Maybe this was all too much, too fast. I admit the "sword in the ass" was maybe a bit much for an introductory photo.

In retrospect, I probably should have gone with the ferret.

I think she would have liked that.

MY JOB MOONLIGHTING AS
"DISH DOLLY R US, INC"

This is one of those times when I actually felt bad after replying to a spam email. Mainly because I don't think this was spam at all, but rather, just some poor guy who somehow got my email address by mistake.

But since you never know if spam is legitimate mail or not, it never hurts to mess with the person on the other side. You know, just in case.

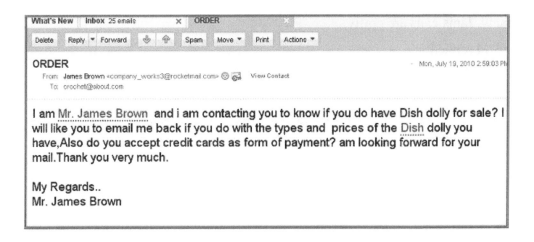

I had no idea what a "dish dolly" was so I Googled it. Originally, I was thinking it was some weird scam thing where James Brown would offer me a million dollars in exchange for a dish dolly, but I would have to wire his deposit on said dish dolly back to him.

BEEN THERE, DONE THAT Mr. James Brown, and you know what they say about "fool me six times" ...

But this is what came up in my Google search:

Oh. Not what you'd base a million-dollar scam on, I think. BUT you never know, Jamaicans are crafty.

So I replied:

```
James,

    I totally have a Dish Dolly. In fact, I have a rather
large selection of Dish Dollys to choose from.

    Are you looking for the standard or deluxe Dish Dolly
model? Prices range from $300 for a low-level Dish
Dolly to $57,000 for the crème-de-la-crème of all Dish
Dollys, "The Liberace."

Let me know.

Williams Schumaker
Dish Dolly R Us, Inc.
```

I figured that was the end of it. Nope.

Thanks for the mail.I will want you to mail me with the cost for the standard once you have so that i can place my order.Do you accept credit card payment? Read from you soon.

This was my first inkling that, no, this was not a scam; it was just some poor shmuck actually trying to buy a Dish Dolly. But if you look at the original email he sent, I was not a recipient, which is a standard ploy for scams. Don't ask me why I know so much about Internet scams. – *sent from my yacht.*

My reply:

James,

Just so you know what you're getting, I'm attaching some brochures for the Dish Dollys we currently carry.

Our middle-of-the-line model, "The Pope Benedict XVI" (we had some technical problems with the XV model) is having some issues getting into the country from Iran due to a higher than normal Uranium content (wtf, Iran), but as soon as we are released from litigation by Homeland Security I will be able to show you that model as well.

Being a new company (two days and counting!), our brochures are still at the printers so instead I'm attaching some of the original sketches of the Standard and Liberace models and I think you'll see, without a doubt, that you'd be better served with the Liberace Model and all its features.

BRAIN NUGGET

YOU KNOW YOU'RE OLD WHEN YOU GROAN PUTTING ON YOUR SLIPPERS.
ALSO, YOU OWN SLIPPERS.

Dish Dolly R Us

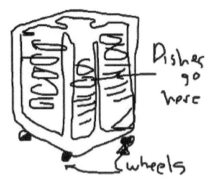

Standard Dish Dolly
$399 plus s/h

Dish Dolly R Us
Standard Dish Dolly description

- made of biodegradable
  styrofoam for lightness and
  ease of throwing
- holds a bunch of dishes
- has wheels so you can ROLL
  IT! (patent pending)
- Includes instructions in
  several languages even the
  most hardened immigrant can
  figure out how to use it *

* standard

Dish Dolly R Us

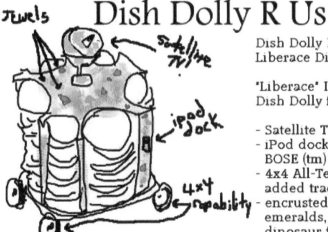

Liberace Dish Dolly
$57,000 plus s/h

Dish Dolly R Us
Liberace Dish Dolly Description

'Liberace' Includes all Standard
Dish Dolly features PLUS:

- Satellite TV hookup!
- iPod docking station with
  BOSE (tm) sound system
- 4x4 All-Terrain wheels for
  added traction!
- encrusted with rubies,
  emeralds, diamonds and
  dinosaur fossils
- Painted in tie-dye colors in
  China

I'm also attaching a picture of a rocket my son drew.

196

```
    To answer your question, yes - I can accept credit
card payment. But only if you use your credit card to
get a cash advance and then mail me the money in an
unmarked, plain manila envelope.


    Cordially your servant,
    William Schumaker
    Dish Dolly R Us, Inc.
```

I never heard from Mr. James Brown again which kind of sucks after all the time I spent trying to get the "Pope Benedict XVI" model to clear customs.

Figures.

Damn Jamaicans.

BRAIN NUGGET

AUTOCORRECT KEEPS TRYING
TO CHANGE "DINGLETWAT"
TO "DONGLE TEAT" AND NOW
I DON'T KNOW WHICH ONE
I LIKE BETTER. :(

THE TIME IN THE FUTURE WHEN I SPAMMED MY PAST SELF AND MAYBE VICE VERSA

This one was a head scratcher.

I honestly have no idea how this actually happened, but I was targeted quite erroneously by this email:

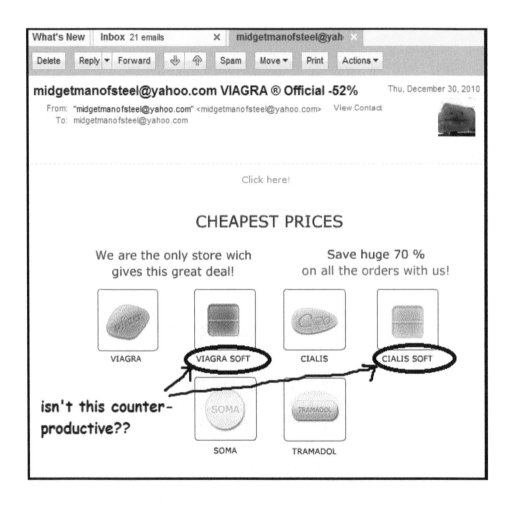

I would normally delete those emails because at the time I was married and sex was a distant memory.

And honestly, I'm still smarting from that time I answered one.

I took the pills they sent me for a month, and grew a labia out of the side of my head. I finished my limit of 32 refills for that order, and stopped responding to those kinds of emails as a whole.

Whole.

Hole.

God, I miss my head labia so much.

But the odd thing that stuck out to me about this email was this:

From: midgetmanofsteel@yahoo.com

To: midgetmanofsteel@yahoo.com

HOLY SHIT.

FROM me. TO me.

Mind? Blown.

It was quite obvious that this email was sent from my future self to warn me that someday I'll be trying to bed Scarlett Johansson, and my dick won't work.

The above photo is not retouched. That is, after I touched it the first time. Hence, the "retouched." Then I decided against retouching it, forcing the "un." I have now completely confused myself. And you too, I'm sure. I'm so sorry.

But now I'm dying to know why I sent myself an email urging myself to order penis medications. Again.

What better way to find out than to ask my future self directly?

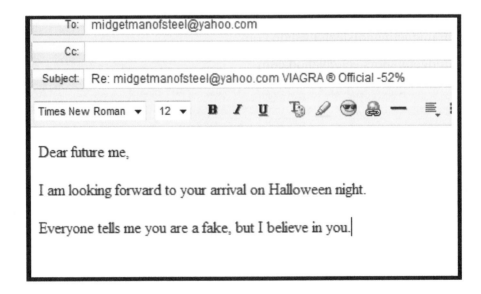

Then I realized I was actually writing to The Great Pumpkin so I started over.

Then I sent it and a few seconds later - BAM - an inbound email from myself showed up in my inbox.

O_O

It was like a Christmas miracle but with less baby Jesus and myrrh. Then I checked the timestamp, and yep, IT WAS SENT FROM MYSELF JUST BEFORE I RECEIVED IT.

Freaky.

If you remember, my full time job is software quality assurance and internet security. And now you now understand why the US is so far behind Asia when it comes to technology and stuff like decent noodle soups.

So, apparently, I was not only my past self, but I was also my future self. But even with all that wormhole stuff going on, I was still in my same pajamas, not banging Scarlett Johansson, and that pissed me off a little.

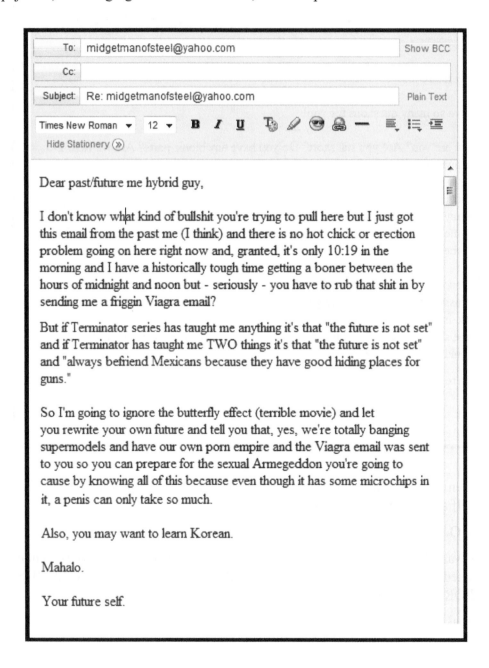

To: midgetmanofsteel@yahoo.com   Show BCC

Cc:

Subject: Re: midgetmanofsteel@yahoo.com   Plain Text

Times New Roman ▾   12 ▾   **B** *I* U
Hide Stationery »

Dear past/future me hybrid guy,

I don't know what kind of bullshit you're trying to pull here but I just got this email from the past me (I think) and there is no hot chick or erection problem going on here right now and, granted, it's only 10:19 in the morning and I have a historically tough time getting a boner between the hours of midnight and noon but - seriously - you have to rub that shit in by sending me a friggin Viagra email?

But if Terminator series has taught me anything it's that "the future is not set" and if Terminator has taught me TWO things it's that "the future is not set" and "always befriend Mexicans because they have good hiding places for guns."

So I'm going to ignore the butterfly effect (terrible movie) and let you rewrite your own future and tell you that, yes, we're totally banging supermodels and have our own porn empire and the Viagra email was sent to you so you can prepare for the sexual Armegeddon you're going to cause by knowing all of this because even though it has some microchips in it, a penis can only take so much.

Also, you may want to learn Korean.

Mahalo.

Your future self.

Then I saved it in my *drafts* folder because I wasn't quite to the "porn empire banging supermodels" point of my life, so sending it would be a bit premature.

Speaking of premature, I should probably tell my past self to buy some of those **Last-Longer** pills, too.

Doesn't hurt to be prepared.

Just ask John Connor.

Technically,
I think these are now
"Dog Nuggets."
You're welcome.

BRAIN NUGGET

MY DOG WON'T STOP DIGGING IN HIS BED. I FULLY EXPECT TO SEE A CHINESE MAN CRAWL OUT ANY MINUTE NOW.

BRAIN NUGGET

MY DOG IS TERRIBLE AT THE "PUNCH BUGGY" GAME. IT'S NOT THAT HE CAN'T RECOGNIZE THE CARS, IT'S THAT HE ALWAYS GETS THE COLORS WRONG.

SPAM GOES THE EASEL

Another email came in one day, this one inquiring about my blog:

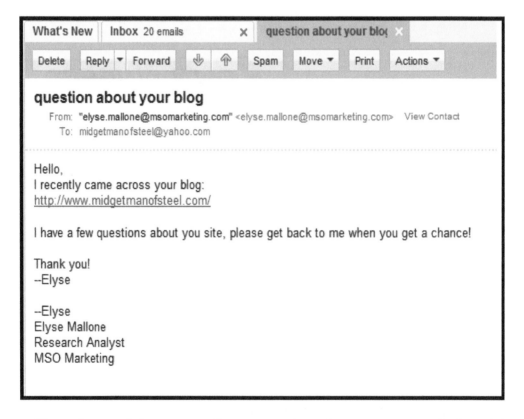

Since the email format was from a template, the grammar was bad, and it was from a woman seemingly interested in me, it was obvious to me this was bullshit. However, emails from women don't come to me very often unless they're accompanying court orders, so I went to their webpage, and saw this:

There were actually no working links on this page other than their "Privacy Policy," which was pretty long. I didn't really read it, but I think it said something like, "our policy is to keep everything we do private."

From: rodney lacroix [mailto:midgetmanofsteel@yahoo.com]
To: elyse.mallone@msomarketing.com
Sent: Wed, 1 Dec 2010 07:38:06 -0800 (PST)
Subject: Re: question about your blog

Hi Elyse,

What kind of questions do you have? Does it have to do with you donating a large sum of cash to me?

I also have some questions about your site, msomarketing.com, too. Mainly because it looks like it's just one page and then a 'Privacy Policy' and the one page has a picture of an easel with a pad of paper so my questions are:

1) Where did you get an easel? Do they even sell those any more? I'm assuming that if you own an easel then you're either a painter from the 1970s or you own a small magic chalkboard.

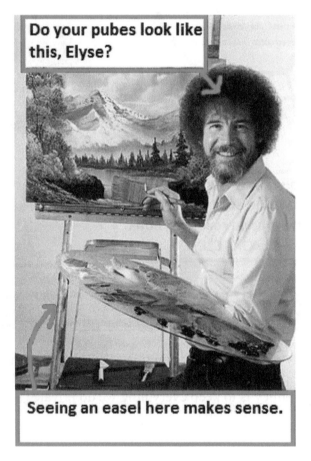

Do your pubes look like this, Elyse?

Seeing an easel here makes sense.

2) If you had a magic chalkboard what would you wish for? I'd wish for more magic chalkboards. Then I'd sell them to people with shitty websites.

3) You list a "7-step" process. Although nowhere on your one page does it list the 7 steps, I'm assuming step 1 is, "Go get yourself an easel."

4) Ever hear of Powerpoint?

I mean, the one guy in the top picture is just pointing at a giant checkmark. He used the WHOLE paper to draw a check mark.

Way to go green, MSO Marketing.

I'm pretty sure Powerpoint has a little check mark icon that you'd just plop right into the presentation. You could probably have the 'Research' guy on your web page do it. His hands look savvy and knowledgeable. He probably puts check marks in presentations in his sleep. He dreams weird things. My magic chalkboard told me this.

Anyway, Powerpoint would probably save you some money in the long run, since you're probably buying shitload of paper and easels and magic chalkboards and stuff.

5) I'm recently divorced. Are you single? I have a free ticket from Southwest Airlines burning a hole in my pocket. I will travel to meet you anywhere in the Continental United States. Except Miami. I watch Dexter and it looks like a lot of people die there. I blame the Cubans. Kennedy was right all along.

Yours in Christ,

Midgetmanofsteel

Re: question about your blog   ·   Wed, December 1, 2010 10:53:36 AM

From: "elyse.mallone@msomarketing.com" <elyse.malli ...   View Contact

To: midgetmanofsteel@yahoo.com

Hi,

Thanks so much for getting back to me! I was wondering if you would be interested in posting a few links on your website directing to Overstock.com? In return we will provide you with a discount code that you can share with your readers.

If you are not familiar with Overstock, they are an online retailer offering everything from diamond rings to sporting goods. And what's even better is they offer 2.95$ shipping no matter what you order!
If this is something you would be interested in please get back to me. Can't wait to hear from you! ?

--Elyse

--Elyse
Elyse Mallone
Research Analyst
MSO Marketing

Way to ignore my email, bitch. My turn!

BRAIN NUGGET

SAW A BEAUTIFUL, MAJESTIC
EAGLE TODAY. AT LEAST I
THINK IT WAS AN EAGLE. I GUESS
I'LL JUST WAIT AND SEE WHAT
THE TAXIDERMIST SAYS.

Elyse didn't send me an easel or magic chalkboard. Instead, she sent me a discount code to put on my blog because no woman can resist the charm of a man asking what your pubes look like over email, especially if it's accompanied by a picture of fish sandals.

FYI, easels can be found under "Crafts & Supplies."

Update: MSOMarketing.com has completely revamped their website; I'd like to take total credit for it because they ditched the easels in favor of springy pie charts. But I'm kind of pissed. Not once do they mention me.

FUDDRUCKERS JUST BURGER BLOCKED ME

We have a hamburger chain here in the Northeast called "Fuddruckers." This is one of the greatest business names on the planet, unless you have children. That's because it's almost impossible to **not** say "Let's go to RuddFuckers!" or sing "Rudd Fuckers, Rudd Fuckers" or make your finger go "rudd fuck ... rudd FUUUCK" while scrawling it on your bathroom mirror with lipstick like you're Danny Torrance in "The Shining."

Kids pick up on things like that.

True story.

Got this from **Fuddruckers** in an email one day:

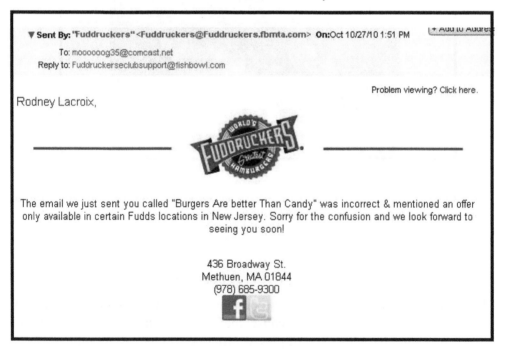

I didn't remember getting the original email they were correcting ... but ...

▼ **Sent By:** moooooog35@comcast.net **On:**Oct 10/27/10 2:36 PM

      To: Fuddruckerseclubsupport@fishbowl.com
      Bcc: rlacroix@enterasys.com

This is bullshit.

Rodney Lacroix

----- Original Message -----
From: "Fuddruckers" <Fuddruckers@Fuddruckers.fbmta.com>
To: moooooog35@comcast.net
Sent: Wednesday, October 27, 2010 1:51:05 PM
Subject: Oops - We Made A Mistake

Problem viewing? Click here.

Rodney Lacroix,

Because you know, nothing pisses a customer off more than being told he doesn't get a special deal he was never offered to begin with. They can go RuddFuck themselves.

* No hamburgers in NJ were harmed during the writing of this story.

BRAIN NUGGET

I SAW A GUY ON A SKATEBOARD
THIS MORNING WITH A FULL BEARD
WEARING SHORTS AND A BASEBALL
CAP, SO I'VE BEEN ABLE TO PUT A
FACE TO 'GIVING UP.'

Bitch, thy name is 'Payback.'

45 years. That's about how long I've been on this planet as I'm writing this.

Roughly 43 of those years have been spent driving people crazy with lies, fabrications, fabricated lies, and getting lye out of fabrics. The latter was due to my days spent toiling in sweater factories at the age of twelve.

My parents didn't believe in child labor laws.

So sure, I've spent the majority of my life giving people a hard time in the name of entertaining myself and others. Sometimes I'll do things not even expecting to see the reaction. Like the time a coworker had Elmo and Pooh Bear stuffed animals on her desk. Every morning I posed them into different sexual positions. I can only imagine that, for her, it was like arriving to a Sesame Street presentation of The Kama Sutra each day.

Today's episode has been brought to you by the letters, "F" and "U" and the number "69."

Yet, there is a reason these sayings exist:

"Payback is a bitch."

"You reap what you sow."

"Have a taste of your own medicine."

You see, one cannot simply go through life playing jokes and pranks and purposely confusing the hell out of people without receiving some kind of payback, eventually. I wish this wasn't true because I'd probably be messing with people at an exponentially greater rate. There should probably be an infinity symbol involved in that equation. Or pi. Or pi AND an infinity symbol. Seriously, it would be crazy.

But what goes around comes around, especially when it involves cyclical references or Frisbees. And when that happens, people WILL turn the tables on you, and you WILL get bitten in the ass.

Just like how I posed Pooh Bear and Elmo that one morning.

RUBBERIZED EW

Arachnophobia

From Wikipedia, the free encyclopedia

Arachnophobia or **arachnephobia** (from the Greek: ἀράχνη, *aráchnē*, "spider" and φόβος, *phóbos*, "fear") is a specific phobia, the fear of spiders and other arachnids such as scorpions.[1]

That?

Yeah. I got that.

I'm not sure why I'm such a massive pussy when it comes to spiders.

I assume it has something to do with their eight legs and four billion eyes and fangs and GAH! I JUST WALKED INTO ONE and swatted it out of midair with hands flailing about like I have some sort of nervous disorder, but now it's on my floor and OH MY GOD LOOK HOW FAST IT'S RUNNING.

burns house down

I saw a spider.
Just to be safe, we should probably burn it again.

Oh my God I almost don't want to write this chapter. But, for the sake of my children and their children's children and the $2 in pure profit I made from you buying this book, I'll suck it up. But I really don't want to.

214

Joe Rogan: "Okay, Rodney. It's down to you and Bill for the million dollar prize. All you have to do to be champion of "Fear Factor", is barely touch this tarantula with a stick."

Me: "Congratulations, Bill."

That being said, I would totally kill a spider if I had to and the conditions were right. Like, if there was a six-foot long newspaper roll in the house and the spider was cornered and couldn't go anywhere and it was already dead. **THEN**, I might be able to approach it.

That's what makes this next chapter one of the worst things my kids could ever possibly do to me.

To the point ... my son bought a rubber spider.

I don't remember where he got it (from hell, I assume) or why he got it or even how I have allowed it to remain in my house except for the fact that I don't want to touch it ...

BUT, he has one. It's big and black and nasty. There is a Forrest Whitaker joke right here, but I refuse to make it. I think I just did. I hope you can forgive me, Forrest.

My children know I don't like spiders. Unfortunately, it seems most everyone else in civilization does too.

On a side note, I have found that in this great big wonderful world of social media, if you happen to mention how much you hate spiders, you will receive – on average – fifty pictures every hour of giant bird-eating spiders on your Facebook wall.

I Googled "rubber spider" for a picture to put here. This came up.

I have no clue wtf is going on here but I'm totally trying this as long as it's acceptable to use Pepsi instead.

Related: I also hate boobs. Thank you in advance.

YUCK. Whatever you do, do NOT send me pictures of boobs like these!

My email is:
midgetmanofsteel@yahoo.com.

Of course, one day, I go to work and head to the break room for a coffee. I open my wallet and as I'm reaching in for a dollar bill there is A GIANT BLACK SPIDER OH MY FUCKING SHIT And ... wait ... wait ... it's just the rubber one. OH thank Christ.

That realization came a little late, unfortunately, as I had already screamed like a bitch in the middle of the cafeteria and my wallet was bubbling in the fryolator because that's where my survival reflex decided to throw it.

Kids: 1

Dad: 0

The next night I stopped by my son's room, bid him a, "Goodnight," and went to tuck my daughter in.

Three seconds later ...

My son screamed bloody murder and came running into my daughter's room and – as payback for me placing the spider on his pillow where he'd see it as he pulled his covers down – punched me square in the kidney as hard as he possibly could.

He continued to punch me while yelling "WHY DID YOU DO THAT?" and then my daughter joined in, and I quickly turned black and blue and began peeing myself because "Let's abuse our father" seemed like a great game to play at 9 p.m.

Kids: 1

Dad: 1

How "Children of the Corn" got started.

As a single dad, I have my kids three or four nights a week, which gives me the opportunity to plan out the attacks a little better than the children. Unfortunately, that also gives them the element of surprise because they have so little time to plan, so I never know what's coming.

Like the morning I lifted the toilet lid and OH MY GOD SPIDER ON THE SEAT!! SPIDER ON THE SEAT!!

Fun fact: It's physically impossible to NOT scream "JESUS CHRIST MOTHERFUCKER!" when you lift a toilet lid and see a spider. Also? WHY DO WE STILL OWN THIS THING?!?!?

Kids: 2

Dad: 1

The spider gag was getting a little old, but the kids needed to learn that their father didn't take things lying down, unless it's ... um ... well, they needed to know their father didn't give up so easily. The next night they stayed over, my daughter found this when she pulled the covers down her bed:

Skadoosh.

That's my trusty childhood ventriloquist doll, Mortimer. If you're wondering why I still have a childhood ventriloquist doll, I can tell you that as an only child you get very, very lonely until you discover masturbation. Or sometimes after. Or sometimes during. Jerking off is a confusing time for me.

BRAIN NUGGET

I ASSUME MY VISA CARD IS HOME ON THE COUCH UNDER A BLANKET WATCHING MOVIES BECAUSE "IT'S EVERYWHERE I WANT TO BE."

My mother gave Mortimer back to me after finding him in some old boxes in her basement. Yes, she still had him from, like, 35 years ago. How Mortimer did not escape his basement shackles and murder her is a testament to the sturdy construction of cardboard boxes when you do that fold-over-fold-under technique with the top flaps.

He probably also realized it would have taken him six hours to crawl out of wherever he was because apparently my mother is a hoarder.

My other doll looked like this. But mine had pants. I'm disturbed on several levels right now.

She also brought over another ventriloquist doll I had as a child that was some hobo clown, but time and bad storage had turned him into a dilapidated creepy clown thing that had no business being in the world, let alone my house.

I threw it in the trash immediately, and as I write this, it's probably clawing its way out of the local landfill trying to return to my house.

double-checks door locks

Needless to say, my daughter lost her mind when she pulled back her sheets, because – you know – ventriloquist doll in the bed.

Kids: 2

Dad: 2

A week or so went by with us trading hidden spiders and ventriloquist dolls and other crap back and forth. This is what we do to pass the time when we're not watching Three Stooges or MMA Fighting.

That said, I believe in giving my kids well-rounded life experiences, and I think Curly or Shemp one night and roundhouse elbows to the throat on another night pretty much covers the full spectrum of childhood memories.

Chicken Soup for the Soul, this is not.

Regardless, as I sat down at my computer table one night, I reached up and turned on the lamp right next to me.

Then I screamed.

Because, well, THIS →

That, my friends, is the black rubber spider ...

Of which my lovely daughter taped to the inside of the lampshade knowing that sometime, someday, I'd turn that damn thing on.

I can honestly tell you that it is still there and, yes, I turn that lamp on every night and YES I still jump and get the chills a little, because GROSS, but it is still there. And as long as it's still there, I know it's not somewhere else.

Like under the toilet lid.

And then there are the times like this gem on the opposite page ... which I found when I went to eat my lunch at work one day.

God I want to kill my kids sometimes.

WHY KARATE IS HARDER THAN IT SHOULD BE

My son and I came home one night from our weekly karate class where we learn things like sidekicks and back kicks and knife hands and roundhouse elbows and how to kill someone using only your wrist. In hindsight it's way less work to just buy a gun.

We also learn how to defend ourselves against attacks from someone armed with wooden staffs. This skill is necessary when you live in Southern New Hampshire and are surrounded by bamboo thickets and fields of sugar cane.

If you're unfamiliar with New Hampshire, we just had a blizzard and my back deck has six-foot snow drifts. So, no bamboo. Or sugar cane.

But you can never be too safe when it comes to defending yourself against an attack involving a long piece of tropical wood.

Assassins are wily.

So, after karate class, my sculpted body glistening with post-karate sweat, I walked into my bedroom and opened my closet door. I reached in, blindly grabbing a pair of sweatpants, and headed to the shower.

A few minutes later, I exited the shower. After five minutes of admiring myself and doing that "tuck" thing that Buffalo Bill does in *Silence of the Lambs* to see what I'd look like as a female bodybuilder, I pulled my sweatpants on.

Or tried to.

They stopped at mid-thigh.

Apparently, I had gained 30 pounds of sheer muscle mass in my thighs at the dojo. Although this would have been cool, it's only happened twice before, and in both of those times I was dreaming.

I looked down at the sweatpants and could see some stitching on the back of them. I rolled the cuff over. There was a word sewn to the butt:

"PINK"

Mother of crap. I must have somehow put my daughter's sweatpants in my own closet.

Towel wrapped around me, I walked back into my room and reached for another pair of sweatpants. That's when I noticed it.

Oh, that little turd.

My daughter, in our absence, switched the entire contents of my closet with hers. All my shirts were gone, replaced with Hollister and Abercrombie and brands I can't afford to buy for myself.

thanks to my mom for purchasing my daughter's wardrobe

My clothes were in HER closet. Well played, little girl.

She was pretty damned proud of herself, too. That is, until I made her undo the damage and switch all the closet contents back to their original states. It took her almost thirty minutes.

> Rest assured, I own nothing pink or orange or with sequins.

On a related note, doing the same work post-prank is *never* as much fun as it is prank-in-progress. So if you ever pull something like this, you should be prepared to be pissed off when your dad responds with "tough shit" and refuses to help you put everything back when you ask him.

Closet contents back in place, I shot her a look of acknowledgement. As she exited my room, I opened my bureau drawer to grab a pair of socks.

It was filled with training bras.

"PAAAYTON!"

She's sneaky. Like a ninja. I should probably watch my back. She may come at me with a stick of New Hampshire bamboo.

GUAPO, THE MAGICAL MEXICAN SHELF ELF

Ah, the holidays. That wonderful time of year when parents perpetuate lies that have been handed down for centuries, so they can go broke buying ridiculously priced electronics and toys that will be sold the following year at a yard sale for roughly 5% of their original purchase price.

My bad wrapping.

My bad rapping.

Doesn't make much sense when I put it that way, does it?

My kids grew up believing in Santa the same way most other Catholic kids did. Every Christmas morning, they'd wake up wide-eyed and wondrous and in about five minutes they'd tear through the $1,500 worth of gifts that took thirteen hours to wrap.

You could always tell the gifts I was in charge of wrapping because they looked like they were packaged by blind elves with a Scotch tape fetish.

We explained to the kids that some of the gifts were wrapped by Santa's "special elves" because even in the North Pole, there's a job for everybody.

After the gifts were torn to pieces, I'd spend the next three hours shredding my fingers into bloody stumps undoing the

500 plastic-wire twisty-tie things inside each box. This was in a valiant effort to free the toy trapped inside, so my children could be bored with it 30 seconds later.

> **Christmas: A cycle of viciousness.**

After my divorce, I was worried about how my children would handle the Christmas season. That is until they realized that Santa would visit EACH HOUSE and – therefore – they would have TWO Christmas mornings. Then theie mantra changed to, "By all means, you two stay separated because ... *CHA-CHING!*"

TIP: Kids handle their emotions quite well when the idea of extra presents is involved.

So it was in December of 2011, with the holidays approaching, my kids came to remind me that the Shelf Elves would be making their annual appearance.

Shelf Elves.

If you're unfamiliar with the concept of the Shelf Elf, you have no idea how fortunate you are. A Shelf Elf is a tiny, creepy little Elf doll that magically appears in your house during the month of December. By "magically appears," I mean "appears after spending $30 on the stupid thing."

Double that amount if you have two kids because each one wants a Goddamn friggin Elf for themselves. So, after watching $60 magically disappear from your wallet, the Elf's job is to hide in a different spot each night until Christmas.

Then each morning, the children wake and go hunting for the damn thing. That is unless the Elf forgets to move because *maybe* the Elf mover had some other stuff on his mind and totally spaced out and went to bed instead of re-hiding the stupid friggin douchebag elf.

Then the Elf mover has to answer to two crying children who think the Shelf Elf really isn't magic at all, or that the Shelf Elf simply hates them.

In a nutshell, Shelf Elves suck the fun out of your house completely.

That's their real magic.

So it was one night in December when my son looked at me and said:

Son: "OH! I have to write my letter to my Shelf Elf!"

Wait. What?

A letter?

I can tell you at this point that in all the years of marriage, my kids had never ONCE written a letter to a Shelf Elf. In turn, the Shelf Elf was not required to write a letter back to said children. It reeked of tomfoolery, I tell you, *reeked*!

Me: "What do you mean? Since when do you do this?"

Son: "Jamie's mom said that if I write a letter to my Shelf Elf, he'll answer it. Jamie wrote one and his Elf answered it. Then I wrote one at mom's house last night and MY ELF ANSWERED IT!"

Of course he did.

Me: "He answers it? How does he answer it?"

Son: "IN GLITTER!"

Me: "In. Glitter."

If you're a mom, and you're reading this, please know that your desire to "go the extra mile" for your child in making their fantasies come true has an adverse effect on EVERYONE ELSE WHO DOESN'T HAVE A GLITTER PEN HANDY AT 8 P.M.

That's right. *I* don't have a glitter pen because (a) I'm a guy, and (b) I forgot to get a new glitter pen when my last one ran out of glitter pen ink as I was bedazzling my cutoff jean shorts.

BRAIN NUGGET

I'M A "DO-IT-YOURSELF"
HOME IMPROVEMENT GUY
IF THE "DO-IT-YOURSELF"
PART INVOLVES FINDING
A CONTRACTOR.

You like?

This is where these holiday legends start biting parents in the ass.

1) Jesus is born
2) Jesus gets myrrh

3) Someone invents Santa. Rumor: Santa brings kids things.

4) Kids tell parents about Santa bringing gifts.

5) Parents are, like, "Ah, shit. Seriously?"

6) Kids get fruit from Santa which is fine because back then citrus was expensive (I have no idea).

7) Kids are happy getting an orange for Christmas.

8) Steve Jobs is born.

9) Steve Jobs isn't happy with IBM; creates Apple.

10) Kids don't want oranges for Christmas unless it's the Fruit Ninja app. They want Apples (the expensive kind).

11) Kids start asking for iPads from Santa.

12) Parents are, like, "Ah, shit. Seriously?"

13) Someone invents Shelf Elf.

14) Kids happy finding hidden Shelf Elf every day.

15) Someone comes up with the brilliant idea that Shelf Elves can communicate and TELLS THEIR CHILDREN THIS.

16) Kids not happy just finding Shelf Elf and now want answers to questions of the Universe written in glitter.

17) Parents are, like, "Ah, shit. Seriously?"

This is what happens when we make things up. Eventually we end up buying expensive electronics and toys while writing to children using a glitter pen and pretending to be a stuffed Elf.

And so, my son wrote out his questions to his Elf and put it near the front door so his Elf would magically answer them.

And, lo and behold, the Shelf Elf answered.

BRAIN NUGGET

KIDS, IF THE TOY YOU WANT FOR CHRISTMAS INVOLVES ME STANDING IN A LINE FOR IT OUTSIDE A STORE AT 6 AM IN 27-DEGREE WEATHER, I SUGGEST YOU START PRACTICING YOUR SAD FACES.

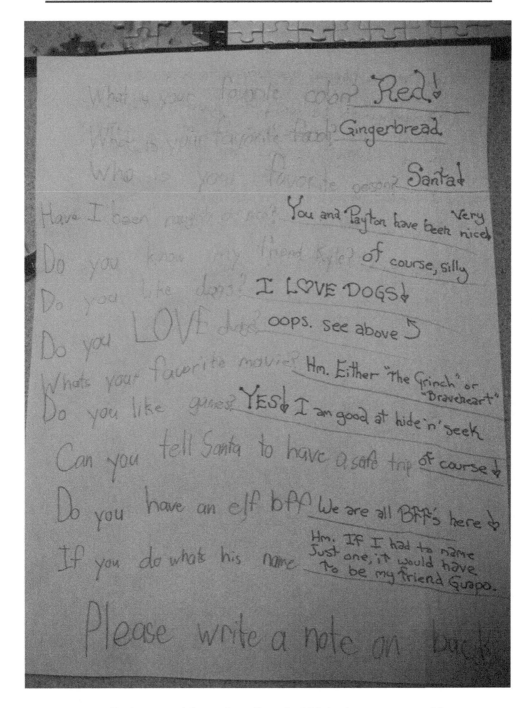

What is your favorite color? Red!

What is your favorite food? Gingerbread.

Who is your favorite person? Santa!

Have I been naughty or nice? You and Payton have been Very nice!

Do you know my friend Kyle? of course, silly

Do you like dogs? I ♥VE DOGS!

Do you LOVE dogs? oops. see above 5

Whats your favorite movie? Hm. Either "the Grinch" or "Braveheart"

Do you like games? YES! I am good at hide'n'seek

Can you tell Santa to have a safe trip? of course!

Do you have an elf bff? We are all BFF's here!

If you do what his name? Hm. IF I had to name just one, it would have to be my friend Guapo.

Please write a note on back.

I was actually happy with my handiwork, if I don't say so myself.

Also, this is about as dainty as my handwriting gets. I normally end all my sentences with little heart exclamations, though. I feel it adds a personal touch, especially on notes left under windshield wipers telling the asshole who parked sideways that I keyed his Hummer.

> **Son:** "The Grinch or Braveheart? What is Braveheart?"

> **Me:** "GREAT movie. Really violent, though. I'm surprised Santa lets him watch it."

Then he gets to the BFF question.

> **Son:** "HAHAHAHA. Guapo the Elf?"

> **Me:** "That actually has kind of a nice ring to it."

Then he flipped it over and read the note on the back:

I am so happy you wrote to me♥

Remember to be good to your friends, your parents, and each other. We are all watching at the North Pole and are very proud of you both.

Meei ← oops♥

Merry Christmas♥

AW DAMMIT.

Yes ... I was in the home stretch of this thing and somehow screwed up spelling *"Merry"* and wrote "Meery" ... as in "Meery Creesmas."

Which, in hindsight, sounds like something my bff Guapo the Elf would say.

TOUCHÉ, MOM. TOUCHÉ.

There's a saying parents tell their kids: "I hope someday you have children who act just like you do." Keep in mind that they usually say this around the time they catch you decorating their expensive fine china with permanent marker or shoving their heirloom jewelry up the dog's asshole.

For the record, writing "fancy dog pooper scooper" on one of mom's fine display dishes and then using said dish as an actual "fancy dog pooper scooper" is good for one week without television.

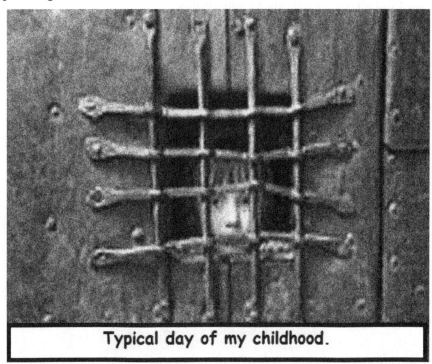

Typical day of my childhood.

I also think the cliché is fairly accurate because children, as a whole, suck the life out of every adult they live with on a daily basis. Kids are like the black holes of society – once you're around one, not even light can escape how frigging annoying they can be.

This is why aunts and uncles and grandparents and single friends love to come visit your children. It's also why when you post on Facebook or Tweet about how awful your kids were that day, these same people comment back, "Aw. Your kids are GREAT. I LOVE YOUR KIDS," and you have to suppress the urge to drive over to their house, knock on their door, greet them with a smile, and punch them in the face.

You see, aunts and uncles and grandparents and friends get to **go home** and leave you and your children behind. They get to drink coffee in the morning and watch the news instead of being subjected to the homo-eroticism of *The Wiggles* or the awesomeness of *Power Rangers*. I mean, um ... yuck. Power Rangers.

whistles and walks away

We, as parents, don't have this luxury. Don't get me wrong, being a dad is one of the few things I'm actually good at that doesn't involve putting swear words into print. But in general, being trapped in a home with tiny little versions of ourselves kind of sucks sometimes.

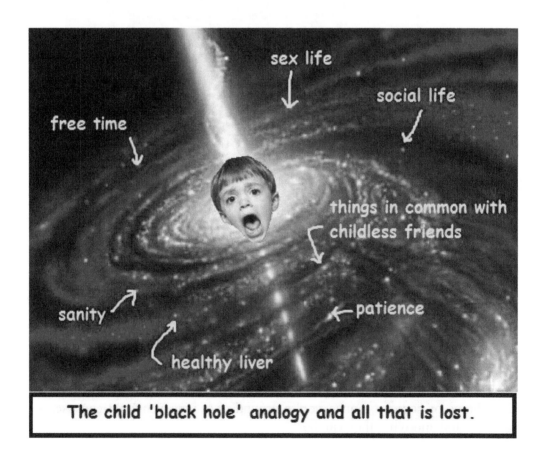

sex life

social life

free time

things in common with childless friends

sanity

patience

healthy liver

The child 'black hole' analogy and all that is lost.

How closely my apple-children remain to my apple-tree became perfectly clear on one evening. I also just realized that the children-tree analogy there is a little creepy. And I also realized that you probably wouldn't have noticed it had I not said anything. So let's pretend I didn't mention anything about children apples and my child-producing apple tree. I'm making it way worse by trying to clarify, so I'm going to stop now.

I was making dinner (read: *using the microwave*) when my daughter – who suffers from the affliction, "I-can't-stop-talking-itis" – began discussing her school day.

> **Payton:** "Dad. Today in social studies we were learning all about public utilities. Electricity. Public Water. Sewerage. Stuff like that."

> **Me:** "Yeah?"

As a sidebar here, I have to ask if I'm the only one who honestly doesn't listen to anything children say. My kids talk about so much so often that my canned response to them is "Yeah?" or "Oh yeah?" or "Okay" or "WILL YOU PLEASE GIVE ME JUST 5 MINUTES?!? I'M TRYING TO GO TO THE BATHROOM" because they will try to talk to me anywhere through any type of barrier.

The 'my kids are talking again' face.

But as parents, I think we're supposed to feign interest in what our children say because it gives them a feeling that they're being listened to and are important and something else probably, but honestly I don't really care.

> **Payton:** "Yep. So we were talking about public utilities and we were talking about where water comes into the house. Can you show me where the water comes in?"

> **Me:** "Um. Okay. Sure."

At this point I'm actually fine with doing this because if my child isn't boring me with something they learned, then I take the opportunity to fill their heads with NEW knowledge. At which point they usually respond with "Yeah" or "Oh, yeah?" or "Okay" and OH MY GOD THEY DO IT, TOO.

Seizing the opportunity to extend my daughter's knowledge of what she learned during the day, I walked her down to the basement – carefully scanning for spider webs because I hate spiders so much I almost want to delete this paragraph since I'm about to type my third variation of the word "spider" in this one sentence.

Also, that was a very long run-on sentence and some people really hate that I write like that. Here's a short sentence:

You're welcome, critics.

No spider webs in sight, I pointed to the corner of the basement and the water service coming in through the wall.

Me: "There it is."

Payton: "Cool. Isn't there a shut-off somewhere? We learned that there is a big valve that turns the water on and off. And there should be a water meter somewhere, right?"

Me: "Yep. Well, the valve is right there" I said this pointing to the yellow handle on the shut-off valve.

Payton: "You just twist it, right?"

Me: "Yep. And there is a meter right outside that measures how many gallons of water we use, and we get charged for it."

Payton: "Yeah. We learned that, too. Cool."

We went back upstairs, confident that I had satisfied the curiosity of my 7th grader with additional information that she wanted. It was like going on a field trip, but we didn't see any animals (thank God) or anything cool, and there were no other moms on the trip chaperoning I could ogle. Now that I'm thinking about it, this would have been the worst field trip ever.

The "water shut-off field trip" goes south.

After dinner, we cleaned up the dishes (read: *threw away paper plates*). The kids headed off into the family room and fired up the TV and their electronic devices while I hopped into the shower.

And then ... 30 seconds into lathering ...

The water stopped.

Sonofabitch.

Son.

Of.

A.

Bitch.

"PAAAAYTON!!!"

The water kicked back on.

I smiled. Then I laughed as I shook my head because THIS? This is what happens when you

AYFKM?!?!?

Even my dog was, like, 'wtf?!'

try to teach your kids something. They turn on you and make you regret it.

So when my mom told me I would have a kid just like me, she was totally right. And when she finished saying it, she went home and watched the news and drank coffee and probably had a hot shower without the water going off.

So jealous.

BRAIN NUGGET

FIANCÉE JUST TEXTED
ME AN AD FOR
"FRESH BALLS FOR MEN."
SUBTLETY IS NOT HER
STRONG SUIT.

MY LITTLE FELON

Concept: Good. **Execution:** Poor.

No, I'm not talking about Anne Heche's foray into lesbianism (Although, if anyone would like to discuss that in detail, we can. Please send pictures to help illustrate your point. Thank you in advance).

I'm talking about those times when you *think* your kids aren't all that smart, and they turn around and fool you.

I believe this phenomenon is similar (but opposite) to when the man of the house purposely screws something up so badly that he is never asked to do that thing ever again.

Like when I was asked to do the laundry one day and decided to dry everything in one big batch on the heat setting of "Lava," thus rendering everything made of cotton able to fit snugly on a Polly Pocket doll. In related news, I actually look good in skinny jeans and yoga pants.

Or the time I was asked to install a ceiling fan in my son's room, and it caught fire. Except that time I wasn't pretending to be incompetent – the ability to accidentally burn down buildings seems to come naturally. I really don't know how to do anything that involves electricity or screws, or honestly, any activity that requires handyman skill at all. My personal hell will turn out to be spending eternity in an IKEA store trying to put together an end table.

But kids? Kids like to make you think they don't have a clue. They pretend to be stupid *on purpose* until you find them constructing a ladder of Legos and chairs and stuffed animals in an attempt to reach a cookie. They pretend because they want you – and everyone around them – to underestimate them.

That way, when it comes time for them to rise up, we won't be expecting it. A lot of parents see greatness for the futures of their children. I see mine trying to kill me in my sleep.

An example of this wiliness happened back when my daughter was seven. My ex-wife received a phone call out-of-the-blue from her teacher.

Pencils had been mysteriously disappearing from the classroom. As it turned out, my daughter was the culprit behind the pencil disappearances – she was caught red-handed taking a pencil from someone's desk.

This came as a shock to me, personally, because I'm pretty sure I taught her how to make sure the coast was clear before ... um ...

I'm pretty sure I taught her the difference between right and wrong.

Caught in the act, the teacher gave my daughter a letter to bring home that explained the situation. She told my daughter that the letter needed to be signed by a parent and returned to school.

The following day, her teacher called her up to the front:

Teacher: "Do you have the letter for me?"

My daughter: "Yep. Here it is."

And she handed her the letter.

The teacher looked to make sure that the letter had been returned signed by a parent, as requested.

It was signed, alright.

It was signed ... just ... like ... this...

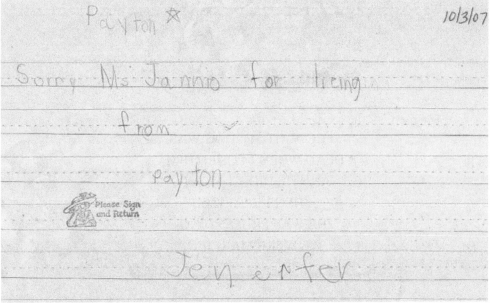

(in pencil)

That sneaky little shit.

I'm not completely clear how, in the mind of a seven-year-old, she thought that would fly. I was so proud of her, though ... just seven years old and already practicing felonies.

I gave her a ten in overall concept, but only a one in execution. Using a pen would have upped her score a bit, maybe to a three.

A more fluid signature with correct spelling would've added at least two more points.

For the record, an illegible squiggle in pen with several loops and dots would have garnered a nine, maybe a ten. So her total score could go anywhere from one to ten, which would be – coincidentally – her possible prison sentence for forgery.

But no one saw her do it. So at least she's learned to make sure the coast is clear before ... um.

Never mind.

BRAIN NUGGET

THOUGHT MY DOG WAS
DEAD WHEN I POKED HIM,
AND HE DIDN'T MOVE.
THEN I REALIZED
HE WAS PRETENDING
WE WERE MARRIED.

THE THINGY

"Vengeance is mine, I will repay, says the Lord." – the Bible

"If you're really a mean person you're going to come back as a fly and eat poop." – Kurt Cobain

"What goes around, comes around" – definition of Karma. Also, carousels.

"God will punish you" – my mother, like, ALL the time

This is the only story in this book that **requires** an introduction.

It is horrific, because – like the rest of the stories in this book – it is true. That said, I really, really wish it wasn't. I've clicked my red ruby slippers together a lot while writing this, yet I'm still sitting here wincing and not in a farmhouse in Kansas surrounded by creepy uncles, discovering it was all just a dream. I knew I should have saved the receipt on those slippers.

It is something that no man – **NO MAN** – should ever have to go through alone. It remains, to this very day, one of the darkest moments of my existence. But, you will probably agree after reading the preceding, that I pretty much deserved every second of it.

You may also wonder **WHY** this story is in this book. It's not a story of me "messing with people." It's not a "how to" of practical jokes.

It's here because I needed to express that all the self-serving shenanigans I've pulled – and that you've just read about – actually **DO** come with a cost. The universe looked down upon me and said "ENOUGH!" And, thus, a terrible penance was rained down upon me from above.

Or below. Depends on your point of view.

You'll see what I mean.

And now ... without further ado ...

As a divorced father of two, I was engulfed in singledom, living a life of virtual bliss. The days I didn't have custody of my kids were filled with Xbox and Playstation and eating crappy frozen meals while watching "How I Met Your Mother." The days **with** my kids were roughly the same, except substitute "How I Met Your Mother" with "Spongebob."

Note to self: Look up the definition of *bliss*.

I was skimming through my part-time parenting existence with relative ease until a couple of years ago. That's when the unthinkable happened ...

My daughter got her thingy.

> **You:** *blank stare*

You know. Her **THINGY.**

> **You:** *blinks, glanced around, shrugs shoulders*

UGH. Her **THINGY.**

THE thingy.

You know, the thingy girls get that comes once a month. Hopefully.

> **You:** *aaah*

Yes. **THAT** thingy.

*gags

NOW you understand.

Yes. The thingy from the toolie.

I should probably note here that I have never once referred to my kids' private parts by their clinical names. I swear that, until the day I die, my daughter's **V** will be called a *"toolie"* and my son's **P** will be called his *"wiggly"* and that thing girls get once a month will be called a *"thingy,"* as in, "Oh. You got your thingy? Dude. So gross."

My fiancée will completely back me up on this. It's one of the main reasons we don't talk about periods or – God forbid – things like yeast infections, which sound much better when they are referred to as "having a Mr. Frothy."

Me: "Did you get your thingy?"

Fiancée: "Yeah. And I also got a Mr. Frothy to go with it."

I don't know why I refer to genitalia as "toolies" or "wigglies." I guess it probably stems from my own youth, when my mother referred to my penis as my "jiggy." On a side note, the song "Getting Jiggy With It" has an entirely different meaning for me, and almost always results in me being tossed out of a dance club.

So, yes, toolies and wigglies and thingies (OH MY) are the norm when speaking of such topics with my kids. But if I don't maintain this semblance of innocence I feel I'll die inside. Bear with me.

So, a few years ago, I got a wonderful text from someone who shall hereby remain anonymous *(threats of defamation lawsuits have some serious pull on book content, FYI).*

The text simply said: *"Your daughter got it."*

Wait. Did I miss something? My daughter got what? Was she up for the main part in a play? Was there a trip to the store for some out-of-stock item she'd been wanting for a while, but I'd neglected to pay attention, because, **HELLO**, she's a girl and guys don't pay attention to girls, **ESPECIALLY** their daughters, because girls are incredibly annoying?

I had no idea what the text meant.

Me: "Got it? Got what?"

Text: "IT."

It? What "it?" What could "it" beeeee ...

Oh. My mind had finally put 2+2 together and came up with the worst answer humanly possible.

IT.

THAT it.

Her ... **THINGY.**

My face went pale. I felt winded and woozy. My spindly legs weakened.

Remember that scene in Star Wars when Obi-Wan said he "felt a great disturbance in the Force, as if millions of voices suddenly cried out in terror?" He would have had the exact same reaction had the Death Star, instead of destroying the planet, simply sent this same text to every single father on the planet of Alderaan.

This pretty much nails my reaction.

Me: "GAH."

Text: "You're going to need to get her supplies for your house."

Whoa whoa whoa ...

SUPPLIES?!

The day was quickly becoming the worst day in history, but instead of having a *"Never Forget"* bumper sticker for it, mine would say *"PLEASE LOBOTOMIZE ME"* because I would have done anything – at that very moment – to have short-term memory loss. And then, on top of the horrific news ... I had to get supplies ...

SUPPLIES ...

Like they were for some sort of sick art project or the worst camping trip in history. Listen, if the supplies you want involve motorcycle parts, paintball guns, or hockey equipment, then I'm your guy.

But the inner workings of the female anatomy and their accompanying leaks, itches, and odors are like the process of making hotdogs: it's gross and I don't want to know.

Just give me the FDA-approved finished product and leave me out of the rest of it. And, yet, there I was, forced to be an unwilling participant in the proverbial hotdog-making process. And I knew what "supplies'" meant in this particular conversation:

Toolie pads and vajayjay torpedoes.

I Googled 'period supplies' and this came up. I have no idea what this has to do with a menstrual cycle but looking at Asian kids in Mickey Mouse hats makes me happier than the alternative.

Me: "OMG can you just get them? Please? I'm begging you."

Text: "Just go and get some pads. She doesn't need tampons yet. I got her some pads called *Tweens*. That's all she needs right now."

aneurism

Me: "Pads? Tweens? Is that a make or model?"

Text: "Just get some regular ones and some overnight ones."

Regular? Overnight? **THEY MAKE DIFFERENT KINDS DEPENDING ON THE TIME OF DAY?!?!**

It was dawning on me I had absolutely no clue how the female anatomy worked, or more precisely, what it took to maintain the damn thing.

Guys? Guys wake up. Guys go to work. Guys go to sleep. Once in a while we pee and sometimes we shave things. But this female stuff seemed like it should come with a fifty-page information booklet.

My mind raced with the instructions I'd been given. Regular pads. Overnight pads. The pads may or may not be called "Tweens." And they were apparently different than tampons.

I wanted to shoot myself in the face. How big were these things?! Wait ... wait ....

Me: "OMG ... seriously ... ARE THERE SIZES?!"

I assumed there were sizes for them. I've seen a ton of porn and some toolies **have** to be larger than others, right? I mean, pads can't be "one size fits all." Everyone knows that when you get something that says "one size fits all," the "all" means "eight-foot tall morbidly obese people."

I've gone camping using one-size-fits-all shirts as tents. We were able to sleep six inside of it and still had room for a stereo. So I assumed that there were S-M-L-XL pad sizes and the XXL ones were in the specialty section and called, "Grand Canyons" or "Just 4 Sluts."

Do you get sized for toolie pads? Is there one of those foot-measuring things hanging around in the feminine hygiene aisle except, you know, it measures your V?

head explodes

Shortly after waking from my catatonic state, I found myself wandering in the Target parking lot alone, afraid, and confused. If I ever have to play the role of a zombie in a movie, I will totally be using "buying pads for daughter" as my motivation. It was also apparent to me that the texter on the other side of this wondrous news was enjoying me losing my mind.

I came to the realization that this was my karmic punishment. I was smack-dab in the midst of a Godly retribution for all the wrongs I'd done in my life. All the lies I'd told, jokes I'd played, and feelings I'd neglected were culminating into this one nightmare of trying to buy feminine napkins for my baby girl.

I stood at the entrance of Target for what seemed like an eternity. After my third blackout, I decided it was time to take the plunge. I ventured down the main aisle, passing the kid's clothing ... the greeting cards ... the movies ... the hair products ... the ... the ...

My pace slowed. My subconscious mind locked up my body.

A lot of time in couples therapy the counselor will tell you that it's not healthy for the parents to stay together for the sake of the child. I'm here to tell the men out there that it actually may be worth staying together just so you don't have to do this kind of stuff by yourself.

Loveless marriage? No sex? Constant fighting? Well, guys, at least you won't have to go search for Tweens in the middle of Target at four in the afternoon on a Wednesday. Just sayin'.

My eyes wandered the aisles. I thought maybe I'd drop by the TV section and **NO! ROD! STAY THE COURSE!** Your little girl depends on you!

And then I turned into **THE AISLE.**

At 5'3" tall, I was dwarfed by two 7' walls of big, poofy packages and multi-colored boxes. I was overwhelmed, like a kid who'd just had

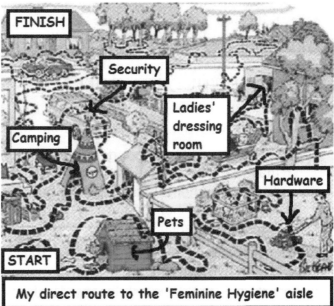

My direct route to the 'Feminine Hygiene' aisle

three Red Bulls, found a bag of quarters, and walked into a Chuck E. Cheese for the first time.

SO MUCH. JUST ... So. Much. It was menstruation overload.

Ah. Thanks for narrowing down my choices, Target.

My eyes searched for ... what did the texts say? I checked my phone – a lot of the texts ended with *"Hello? Are you there?"* because I had apparently been in a self-induced coma for twelve straight hours.

Ah ..."Tweens."

I quickly scanned the aisle. Up. Down. Left. Right. Zig zag and diagonal. My eyes hadn't had this much exercise since I searched for nipples in the last Sports Illustrated Body Painting Swimsuit Edition.

Tweens ... Tweens ... Tweens ... **OMFG I CANNOT FIND "TWEENS" AND WILL SOMEONE PLEASE HELP ME?!**

A woman walked into the aisle, and I glanced at her with a "help me" puppy-dog stare; but seriously, what was I going to ask her?

> **Me:** "Hi ... my little girl got her ... you know (*points at crotch and makes explosion effect with hands and goes *pooosh**) ... and I need to get her these things ... I guess ... and will you do me a favor (*hands her my car key*) and just slice my jugular open with this? Thanks."

At that point I felt like James Franco in ***127 Hours***, stuck under that boulder and knowing deep down that I was really on my own, and **NO ONE** was going to help me find *"Tweens"* for my daughter's thingy, and I would've seriously considered cutting my arm off if God would just make her thingy hold off for another, like, seven years or something when she could shop for this shit herself.

Please, God, please. Just let me find these things and I swear I'll be a good person and go to church every Sunday and never tease people or lie or swear again.

The blatant lie in the previous sentence doesn't count. God's heard that one many times before, and I'm pretty sure he allows us to promise him stupid things that we'll never live up to in times of desperation. Like when we're throwing up from too much drinking or lost in a store trying to find maxi pads.

That's when I spotted them.

The *"Tweens."*

The **LAST BOX** of *"Tweens."*

I snatched it up like I was Gollum grabbing that damn ring, and then I wished it *was* that ring because I would have totally put it on and become invisible.

YES. My precious Tweens.

I was so excited I considered slamming the box of Tweens to the floor like I'd just made a touchdown. Then I thought better about it because (a) it was the *last box* of Tweens, and (b) I didn't know if there was anything breakable in there.

Tweens checked off, I looked for the *"overnights."* Only two makes of those things appeared to be *"overnight pads,"* and based on the size of the soft packaging, they were constructed for use on African Elephants.

They had to be at least a foot long and could probably be used as floatation devices in emergency situations.

I spun around and stared at the opposite wall.

SO MANY PADS. Nope ... no overnights over there. Wait ... some of them said, "Wings?" **Do I get wings?!** Why do they make flying ones? Were they for pilots? I don't think I'd ever been so confused in my life.

> **Me:** "Okay. Got one box of Tweens. The overnights though ... they look huge. Wings? Do I get wings?!"
>
> **Text:** "No. No wings."

I looked at the boxes again, and the only overnights I saw had wings. I'd jumped the gun on the "wings" question. Now what?! I was explicitly told, "No wings," but all the overnights were winged.

Well, crap. Whether she liked it or not, she was going to get wings. Right then I wished I had wings because I would've flown right the hell out of there.

I grabbed a package of overnights, tucked it under my arm with the Tweens, snatched a Harley Davidson magazine just to even everything out, and headed to the checkout.

DONE.

I went home, cleared out a drawer in the bathroom, put all my girl's *"supplies"* in it, closed it, ran to the other end of the house, and jumped on the sofa, crouched in the fetal position. As I closed my eyes and tried to wash away the events of the day, a deep, booming voice echoed in my head:

"Gotcha."

Then it hit me.

For the past sixty years – four generations – the Lacroix line had been nothing but boys. Not one single girl had donned the Lacroix name unless she'd married into it.

Until me.

And why? Because karma had been saving up for this very day, when I would be forced to buy "supplies" for my girl in what could only be described as a personal hell. This was payback for all the times I'd messed with people.

Touché, God. Touché.

Still shaking my head in disbelief, I flipped through the Harley magazine I'd bought, and I found a new seat for my bike because the padding on mine was becoming a little thin.

Padding.

Pad.

retches

God, I wish I'd had two boys.

BRAIN NUGGET

MY DAUGHTER'S MUSIC LIBRARY IS SYNCED TO MY IPOD. DIDN'T REALIZE IT UNTIL I FOUND MYSELF CRYING IN THE CORNER OF THE GYM LISTENING TO ADELE.

Epilogue

Shortly after writing this book, Rodney Lacroix tragically died in a freak snowshoeing accident.

Actually, no I didn't.

waves from bushes

I apologize for freaking you out and scaring you and maybe forcing Scarlett Johansson to scream out, "NO GOD! WHHYYYY?!?" in a hotel room at 3 a.m.

No, it's really me here writing this. However, I've been sitting here for so long trying to figure out what to write that I ended up Googling "What do I write in an epilogue of memoirs?" which led me to these on Yahoo Answers:

pongpresario answered 5 years ago

Silly boy. The epilogue is written by someone else after you are dead.

 1   3   Comment

Pete answered 5 years ago

Unless you're already dead, you probably don't want an epilogue to memoirs.

 1   1   🗩 Comment

Ah, crap.

Epilogues: being done wrong by people who are alive since people who are alive started writing epilogues.

Well, I'm technically NOT dead, although right when I turned 45 I pulled my back doing a sit-up. I have no idea how you pull a back muscle while doing a simple stomach exercise, but I'm pretty sure that's an indication I'm not too far off from the sweet, sweet release of death.

```
    Dear Scarlett, you best get your ass over here soon.
There's no telling how long I'm gonna hold on at this
rate.
```

pops Levitra and stares longingly out front window

So I started to think about what other people would write as my epilogue if I wasn't here to write it myself. Sadly, everything I thought of ended up looking something like this:

Epilogue

Rodney Lacroix was an ASSHOLE.

fin

Damn. And that's the good one I could use without swears in it. From my mom.

So, you know, THAT'S not good. It's completely true, but not exactly the legacy I want to leave.

Although this book is FULL of stories of me jerking people around and messing with heads and lying and generating a waiting line at the gates of Heaven not seen since Lucifer disguised himself as the Pope and tried getting back inside circa 1946, the book doesn't have ALL of the stories.

In related news, I'm a terrible, terrible Catholic.

For instance, I didn't include the story about when my friends and I got jobs at a local air show. We were stationed at the entrance to sell full-color programs. So we stood there like morons, holding programs, watching all the other people who watch air shows stroll in and walk right by us.

It was at that time I decided to step up my sales pitch by opening the programs and pretending to make the airplanes fly.

IT WAS GENIUS.

I made airplane noises and made the plane pictures go UP and DOWN and vroooom and programs were literally flying out of my hands.

That's when my sales pitch turned to this: "GET YOUR PROGRAMS HERE! BUY ONE! GET ONE!"

A giant burly man walked up to me and gave me money for a program. As I handed him the program and said, "Thanks!" he furrowed his brow and glared at me.

"Where's my other one?"

"Um," I said. "What other one?"

"You said, 'buy one, get one.'" he snapped back.

To which I replied, "You bought one. And you got one. Dude, I didn't say they were FREE."

Shortly after pulling that crap, Rodney Lacroix tragically died from being stuffed into the engine of a Cessna with an airplane show program sticking out of his ass.

Honestly, I'm sure you're just as surprised as I am that I'm writing my own epilogue. And in that, I'm VERY truthful.

Stick a needle in my eye.

Man, another needle. This eye is getting mighty crowded.

And I leave you with the number one reason to never let your children help you make out the grocery list ...

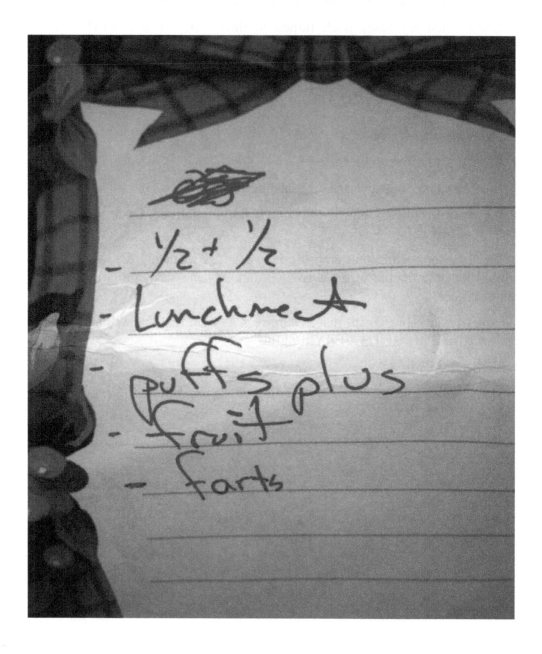

About The Author

Rodney Lacroix is a comedian, father of two amazing kids, reluctant 40-hour-a-week software engineer and best-selling author. In 2013, Rodney was awarded an NGI Book Awards Medal for his memoir, "Things Go Wrong for Me." This beautiful medal is currently on display around his neck because he has not taken it off since receiving it. Also he's not very humble.

Rodney firmly believes that fabricating grandiose tales about one's self makes a person more impressive. That's exactly what he told Playgirl Magazine when they did a 4-page nude spread of him.

It's probably best you don't believe anything Rodney says.

You can find Rodney at MidgetManOfSteel.com and DumbECards.com.

Also from Rodney Lacroix ...

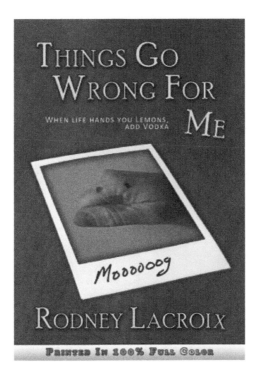

FINALIST - 2013 Next Generation Indie Book Awards (Humor)

FINALIST - 2013 National Indie Excellence Book Awards (Humor)

"As a middle-aged woman, I can safely declare that Rodney's *Things Go Wrong For Me* is targeted to pre-pubescent boys with a penchant for juvenile delinquency and a fistful of Twinkies. Two words: I loved it."

- **Margaret Andrews,**
Author of *Nanny Goats in Panties* and *Sticky Readers*

"A hysterical book written by a man with no filter, a vasectomy and a name like 'Rod?' I'm all over it."

- **Jenny McCarthy, NYT Bestselling Author,**
TV personality, Cougar Raper

CPSIA information can be obtained at www.ICGtesting.com
Printed in the USA
LVOW02s0833181213

365859LV00003B/7/P